MAREK HLASKO

the eighth day of the week

TRANSLATED FROM THE POLISH

BY NORBERT GUTERMAN

GREENWOOD PRESS, PUBLISHERS
WESTPORT, CONNECTICUT

Library of Congress Cataloging in Publication Data

Hłasko, Marek.
    The eighth day of the week.

    Translation of Ósmy dzień tygodnia.
    Reprint of the 1st ed. published by Dutton, New York.
    I. Title.
[PZ4.H678Ei4] [PG7158.H55]   891.8'5'37   74-27462
ISBN 0-8371-7896-7

Translated from the Polish ÓSMY DZIEŃ TYGODNIA

Originally published in 1958 by E. P. Dutton & Co., Inc., New York

Reprinted with the permission of the publishers, E. P. Dutton and Company, Inc.

Reprinted in 1975 by Greenwood Press, a division of Williamhouse-Regency Inc.

Library of Congress Catalog Card Number 74-27462

ISBN 0-8371-7896-7

Printed in the United States of America

the eighth day of the week

the eighth day of the week

1

"No," Agnieszka said. Firmly, she pushed his hand away, and drew her skirt tight around her. "Not now."

"Have it your way," the man said. He lay beside her on the grass, staring at the opposite bank of the Vistula. In the middle of the river, a comical tug-boat was laboriously towing three heavy barges, its engine pumping as hard as an old man's heart. Night was falling, the cold air solidifying like milk. The trees grew darker. The man lay motionless until he felt Agnieszka's hand on his head.

"Pietrek, I don't want this to be cheap," she said quietly. "If I didn't love you, perhaps I wouldn't care. People might come along. I don't want others walking all over something that's important to me. You've got to understand. If there's anything we have to protect, surely it's this."

He raised himself on his elbows, and lifted his face. She had to close her eyes: his youthful features, pure as a child's, were twisted with pain.

"Agnieszka, do you know how terrible it is to beg for it?" he said. "Do you know what it means to wait?"

"I'm waiting too."

He grasped her hand. His eyes were now close to hers—they were dark and had a fixed expression. "How long must we wait? It's hell."

"We must wait," she said averting her eyes. The tugboat had now been swallowed up in the mist. "Maybe we can get an apartment. In the summer we could go away. . . . You don't want it to be in some shabby room or on a park bench, do you?"

"No."

They fell silent. Over their heads the sky was turning golden; the river too was gold. Drops of dew had appeared on the grass, and though they were sitting on his leather jacket, Agnieszka shivered. The opposite bank disappeared in the gloom.

"I've been lying," Agnieszka said suddenly, and he detected a note of suffering in her voice. "I can't wait any longer. I don't care. But at least try to get a room, four walls. Anything—but not here. Not in public. Do you understand?"

"Yes," he whispered. He touched her hand: it was icy, closed like a shell. He sighed and said: "Let's go. It's dark."

They rose. They went through the entire Bielany Woods in silence; only when they reached the street-car tracks, did he say: "I'll speak to Roman, he's got a room. Let him go somewhere else for one night."

"You'll speak to Roman," she thought. "I know what you'll tell him. You won't tell him that you love me and that I love you. You'll say to him: 'Roman, I've got a girl, I need a place to do it. Lend me your room for one night.' And he'll ask: 'I hope at least, she's pretty? You'll make a face, and wink, and say, 'How do I know? It's off season, so what am I to do?' You won't say anything, for you too want to protect this thing. And then both of you will make a few other dirty remarks, even though you've had pitifully few women, and know absolutely nothing about them."

There were only a few passengers in the streetcar —two old women, a sad-faced soldier, and a couple of teenage boys with a soccer ball. The lighted houses sped backward into the dark. Agnieszka smiled and pressed close to Piotr.

"All right, Pietrek," she said. "Speak to Roman."

"What's today?" he wondered aloud. "Thursday?"
"Yes, Thursday."

"I'll ask him to go somewhere else for Saturday night." He touched her ear with his lips. "So long, Agnieszka."

The streetcar stopped. The conductor looked over his glasses and announced through his nose: "Railroad crossing." Pietrek squeezed Agnieszka's hand and jumped out. She followed him with her eyes: he was as slender and lithe as a hazel tree. He walked with his head down. "Why does he stoop like that?" she thought. "My God, suppose he doesn't speak to him, after all." After a moment he was lost in the evening crowd. The first stars were just beginning to emerge over the city; only the Great Cross, in the very middle of the sky, gleamed fully and steadily.

"Targowa Street," the conductor announced. She raised her coat collar: a warm rain was beginning to fall. Two men in working clothes were walking ahead of her. One of them swore, saying to the other: "It's pouring again. It's a long time since we've had such a filthy May. You can't even take a girl into the bushes." "Who for instance?" the other said. "My mother-in-law, maybe. Got any money?" When Agnieszka passed them, he jostled her with his elbow, and said to his companion: "Would you do it with her?" "I wouldn't mind," the first said, "but she won't give it to guys like us." "Maybe we should ask?" the other said, and he cried: "Hey, I'll go with you. . . ."

She left them behind, and turned into Brzeska Street. Drunks were reeling in the murky circles of light under the street lamps. A drunk was bounced out of the "Sailors' Haven" bar and fell on his face on the sidewalk; a moment later his hat and briefcase were flung out after him. Small groups stood gaping in the doorways without a word; a bass voice was blaring over a loudspeaker: "Today's sprint ended with the defeat of the Polish team. The first to reach the goal was the Rumanian Dumitrescu . . ." From the market came the stench of rotting vegetables. Someone was singing in a shrill tenor. A young boy looked into Agnieszka's face and whistled. Another one murmured wistfully, "Christ, she'd screw like a dream." Cats roamed about her feet; the stars vanished in the mist. A drunk whispered hotly into her ear: "The old lady's out of town. I have the place to myself. I'll give you some nylons, how about it?" At the East Station locomotives were tooting; only with difficulty could she get the damp air into her lungs; the faces of the passersby were sweaty and their eyes were glazed.

"Do speak to him," Agnieszka said to herself. "Speak to him as soon as possible."

2

At home her father asked her: "Where have you been, Agnieszka?"

He was standing by the window, looking at the street through a crack between the curtains; he could stand thus for hours on end watching what was going on outside. He was short, balding, older than his years; he had an unhealthy complexion and faded eyes. He was an inspector in a co-operative union; the only times he came to life were when he managed to uncover some malpractice.

"I went for a walk," Agnieszka said. She took off her raincoat and hung it in the hall. Then she came back. "Has anyone been to see Grzegorz?"

"No," her father said, continuing to drum on the window with his fingers.

"Do you believe her, that she went for a walk?" the mother asked jeeringly from her bed. She would lie in bed for days at a time, an unattractive, soured woman, with a tendency to hysteria and a weak heart. "Do you believe it?" she repeated. "I bet she's been out fooling with some fellow." She turned her perennially swollen, pale face to Agnieszka. "You'll get what's coming to you," she said in an aching voice. "But I don't want a kid here."

"You didn't ask me if I wanted to be born," said Agnieszka. She lighted her night lamp, took out some books, and sat on her bed in the corner with her legs pulled under her, and her chin on her fists. "I want to study," she said.

"Study, study," her mother said with a groan, her face wearing an expression of martyrdom. "Grzegorz studied too, and what came of it? You'll end up like him, if you don't come to your senses."

"I'm of age."

"But I feed you," her mother said. Her voice was tearful now, and her husband turned away. "I'm the one that feeds you, nobody else," she repeated.

"The way you cook," said Agnieszka, "you shouldn't mention it. Now let me study."

"Agnieszka, Agnieszka," her father said. His voice had no body, and now, when he tried to speak severely, he only sounded ridiculous. He wrung his hands, and looked at her reproachfully. "How can you talk back to your mother that way? Your mother who brought you into the world."

"Are you sure the world is so beautiful that I should be thankful to her?" Agnieszka said. She rose, throwing down her books with a thud. She walked over to the window and stood next to her father. "I wish there were no drunks, no streets like this, and . . ."

"And what?" her mother asked aggressively.

"That's easy, no people like you." She turned to her father. "Has Zawadzki come back?"

"No," her father said. He hunched up, gazing at Agnieszka with the eyes of a dog. "He comes home late, you know."

"I'll study in the kitchen," said Agnieszka. She gathered up her books and walked to the door. Before going out she stopped. "I'm sorry, Mother," she said slowly. "Sometimes my tongue runs away with me, and then I'm sorry."

"Better watch out for yourself," her mother said. She gave another groan. "I'm sure you're going out with some good-for-nothing, when you should be staying home." She began to speak faster and with emphasis: "But I'm not going to set up a nursery here—merciful Jesus, who could have foreseen all this? . . ."

Agnieszka gazed at her in silence, and walked out. She went into the kitchen and turned on the light. The kitchen was small and cluttered; the beds took up a great deal of room. One belonged to her brother Grzegorz; the other to Zawadzki, a mechanic employed by the Warsaw Gas Works, who had been staying with them since 1945, still waiting for an apartment of his own.

She sat at the table and spread out her books. With an effort she read half a page, then her father came into the kitchen. He stood in the middle of the room, and cleared his throat, shifting his weight from one foot to the other. She looked at him questioningly.

"Agnieszka, what's the matter with you?" he said.

"What do you mean?"

"What's Mother talking about?"

"It's obvious. I'm a streetwalker. Tell Mother I said so. Is that enough for you?"

"Agnieszka," her father said imploringly. "Agnieszka . . ." He looked at her helplessly. "I'm afraid Grzegorz will come to a bad end." He spread his hands. "Why don't we understand each other at all?"

"We understand each other perfectly," said Agnieszka. "The poor woman's sick, the apartment's small, you earn practically nothing. And now go back to the living room, otherwise Mother will suspect you of plotting something horrible with me."

He was sitting down now. He folded his hands on his knees, gazed at them pensively, then raised his head.

"I'm getting old," he said. "Sometimes I feel terribly tired. Mother's always sick, Grzegorz drinks, and you're so strange . . ." He smiled at her timidly. "I'd like to know how you are getting along," he said. "Can I help you somehow?"

"No one can be helped, really helped," she said. She pushed back her heavy bronze hair and was silent for a while. She saw that he was staring at her fixedly. "Each of us has to help himself," she said. "Anything else?"

He sighed.

"Next Sunday I'll go fishing," he said. "I want to relax a bit, and I can't do it here. I've got my rods ready; now I must still get a line, and that's not easy these days. Shall I go to Piaseczno? Or where I was last year, out by Wolomin? There are marl pits there." He gave another sigh. "It's still a long time to Sunday."

"Three days," she said. "That's not much."

"Three days," he echoed her. He smiled. "My God, three days. You can't imagine how many things can happen in three days. It's a terribly long time."

"What's three days compared to a whole lifetime?"

"A great deal. Sometimes you can lose everything in three days."

"I don't think so, but never mind. Take my advice, go back to Mother."

He rose. "So where should I go, Agnieszka? To Piaseczno or Wolomin?" He gazed at her intently.

"To Wolomin, of course."

"I guess that's what I'll do," he murmured. "Thanks."

He walked out. It was stuffy: Agnieszka opened the window. After the rain the air was as pure as a child's breath. The street was not yet asleep. Almost all the windows were open, and from almost all of them came the nasal tones of the loudspeaker: "With justifiable pride it must be emphasized that we have won a victory in our struggle against the cult of the individual, so harmful in its consequences, so conducive to deviations. Now we must proceed to cut it out by the roots. The directives of the Twentieth Congress must become . . ."

"If it were possible to forget," she thought, covering her face with her hands, "if it were possible to forget all that. Peace. A little peace and quiet. Nothing more. No Pietrek, no Father, no Grzegorz. Just peace and quiet. Let anything go on elsewhere, but where I am, let there be only peace and quiet. That is all, yes, that is absolutely all. . . ."

She raised her head and again looked over to the opposite side of the street. In a window on the second floor a fat man in an undershirt was shaving, his lips twisted comically. The radio was blaring: "Then night will come, which is our destiny." A tractor passed making a monstrous noise. Someone came into the kitchen, and Agnieszka turned. It was Zawadzki, a man in his thirties with a healthy complexion and blue eyes. His colored shirt was unbuttoned down his chest; his neck was hard and strong.

"Good evening," he said. He took off his coat and hung it carefully on a chair. He poured water into the basin and began to roll up his sleeves; his arms were deeply tanned.

"Going out?" asked Agnieszka.

"That's the thing to do," he said cheerfully. "No

point staying at home on such a fine night. How about you?"

"I have to study," she said. "That's why I've invaded your stronghold. The parents fight all the time."

"What else have they got to do?" he said, grinning. "At their age all they can do is either fight or play chess." He rubbed himself with the towel so hard that his body took on the color of freshly-baked bread. "Buy them a chess set," he said, "and you'll have peace and quiet at home."

"Where are you off to?" she asked. She wished he would go now.

"To my friend's. We'll finish our work on that engine."

"That motorcycle of yours!" Agnieszka said, smiling. "It's all you talk about. Some day I'd like to see you ride it."

"I have to change the clutch," he said with some irritation. He threw down the towel, sat on his bed, and proceeded to change his shoes. For a moment he struggled with the shoelace, then raised his head. "You wouldn't be so sharp either if you had to put up with the same rider for ten years. Do you think you're smarter than my engine? I'll fix the clutch, and Sunday I'll go to visit my fiancée."

"Don't get mad. You've been saying that for the past three weeks." She sat on the windowsill, swinging her legs. "I'm curious to see what will happen then."

"Listen, Agnieszka," Zawadzki said. "If they're writing me the truth, if it's true that she's betraying me, I'll fix her face so that no hospital will admit her."

"And then?"

"I don't know."

"Do you love her?"

"More than you think."

"Then why do such a stupid thing?"

"Because."

"If you didn't love her, what would you do?"

"That's easy: I'd go on living with her."

"So what good will it do you?"

"A great deal."

She shrugged, and leaned out the window. People were brawling on the street before the entrance to a store. "I'll show you who's got a brother in the secret police!" someone roared. The sky looked into Agnieszka's eyes with two faces—its own and that of the puddles; both above and below, the stars were tiny, unreal. Agnieszka started: Zawadzki had put his hand on her arm. She looked at him and only now noticed for the first time that the man standing before her had a bitter mouth, and that there were hard lines on his forehead.

"Listen," he said. "All of you are basically the same, and that's why there's actually no point talking with you. But I'll tell you one thing: a man wants to have something for himself alone, and you can't change that. If he can't have a friend or a girl like you, he wants at least to preserve his beggarly sense of honor. When we were at the Oflag, one of our boys got a letter from his family saying that his girl was going out with Germans. We were so bored in the camp that everybody teased the boy mercilessly. 'It's nothing, Mietek,' they told him, 'don't take it so hard. After you go back home and marry her, hang a print of the *Battle of Grunwald* over your bed. You'll feel better whenever you look at it: that time, *we* licked *them*.' The boy was going wild from frustration. Finally he said, 'Never mind, I'll teach her a lesson.' 'And what if this is a Thirty-Years' War?' 'I'll take care of her in two weeks,' he said, and next day he was gone. We covered up for him for a month, and then he came back. 'I've done it,' he said. Well, Agnieszka, he crossed three borders twice, because he had to go a roundabout way, for the sole purpose of killing her. He did it with a broken bottle ———

you can imagine. He was a madman, that's
certain, but I liked him better than some I've
known."

He walked away from her. He took a coat from the
closet and put it on.

"What became of him?" Agnieszka asked.

"That boy, you mean?"

"Yes."

Zawadzki's smile wasn't pleasant. "Well," he said,
"he got no pleasure from what he'd done. After all,
he might have got a gun and put an end to her. He
seemed to have lost his mind. He walked about the
camp saying, 'I satisfied her for life.' In the end he
cut his throat with a razor in the latrine. Good night,
Agnieszka. Where's Grzegorz?"

"I don't know," said Agnieszka. "Must be drinking
somewhere."

"Is he still waiting for her?"

"Still."

"That, too, is a fine thing," said Zawadzki. "Good
night."

He walked out; his steps echoed loudly on the stairs
—he took several steps at a time, like a little boy.
The street brawl was ending. The drunks now had
their arms around each other. "And why do you do
such things to me, Witek?" one of them blubbered.

He had a young voice. "That's life," the other one said. "In that case, everything's all right," a third man concluded. He drew them to him and introduced them to each other: "Get acquainted, gentlemen: an old army pal—a school pal." "Ah," said the first and began to giggle. "Ah . . ." Arm in arm the three of them stamped out the stars in the puddles.

"The end," Agnieszka thought. She closed the window and sat at the table.

Her father came into the kitchen. He was wearing a motley costume—an old homespun topcoat, a dark hat, a cotton scarf. "I'm going to get Grzegorz," he said, "Mother is having hysterics."

"Where will you look for him?" Agnieszka said. She walked up to her father. She was taller than he, and seemed stronger. Next to her he looked like a dry bush alongside a sapling. She stared at him for a while, then her clear eyes suddenly went out, like a spark covered by a hand. "You're planning to drag him out of some bar?"

"Yes," he said. He shifted his weight from one foot to the other and put his hands behind his back. He tried to look resolute. "I'll drag him out of his bar," he said, "and I'll give him such a talking to that he'll not want another drink for a long time."

23

"Stefan!" her mother cried in a weak voice. "Are you on your way?"

"Yes, dear, I'm going," he said. He adjusted his hat and took a step toward the door.

"Just a minute," said Agnieszka. She walked over to the door and shut it.

"If you find him at all," she said. She forced her father to sit on a chair, and took his hat from his hand. "It won't be easy," she said. "Nor will your talk be of any help. Tomorrow he'll drink again. Don't bother him."

"Why?"

"He's completely alone now."

"Why?"

"He's in love."

"But he has parents, a home, a sister."

"He has nothing except torment."

"What torment?"

"It's his business, not ours."

"So I'm supposed to sit at home and wait calmly while my son is knocking about in bars!" He rose and reached for his hat. He banged his fist on the table. "Devil take it," he said. "I'll bring him home if I have to drag him!"

"Home," Agnieszka echoed. "Home—where Mother does nothing but groan and you sit with a pencil figuring that fifteen years ago you could buy sixty quarts of vodka on your pension, while now it scarcely comes to twenty. Home, where he has no corner for himself. To this day his parents can't understand how they have managed to be bored with each other for twenty-odd years! Home! why, here there's no real difference between the crucifix and the portrait of Stalin, for none of us understands either of them. This is the home you want to bring him back to?"

He was silent. He sat motionless, his head lowered. He clasped his hands together on his knees and squeezed them so hard that they turned white, like the hands of a dead man.

"What am I to do?" he said after a moment. He reached for his hat, then put it down again. "What am I to do?" he repeated. "I'd like to do what's best for you."

"Don't stoop," she said. "Sunday you'll go fishing. I'll go to get Grzegorz."

She took his hat from his hand, and went out to the hall. She put on her coat, pocketed the house keys. Her father said imploringly: "Come back soon. . . . God, I wish it were Sunday already. . . ."

"If she comes for Grzegorz," Agnieszka said, "ask her to leave a note for him."

"Agnieszka," said her father, "will she ever come?"
She stopped in the doorway. "No."

She walked out into the street. The sky had turned completely dark. The city was falling asleep, sprawled motionless under the sharp brilliance of the stars.

3

"He's here," the doorman said with a smile for Agnieszka. There was a wide gap between his two front teeth, and it somehow gave his face a roguish air. "At the bar. How will you get through to him? There's such a crowd tonight. . . ." He walked away toward a noisy party of new arrivals.

Agnieszka went inside. The room was dark and stuffy; star-shaped bulbs gleamed in the low ceiling. She was obliged to stop near the dance floor; the couples crowded into a few square yards stepped on each other's feet and continually bumped into each other, apologizing and exchanging greetings. The women were all dressed alike, and all perfumed with the same cheap *Poem*. They had their heads on their partners' shoulders, a cloud of smoke hovered under the ceiling, the curly-headed vocalist was mumbling tearfully something about separation. One of the waiters said to Agnieszka, "Step aside please, you're in the way . . ." He looked at her face close up. He was young, handsome and dark, gleaming with brilliantine and a gold tooth. "Yes," he said sorrowfully, "that's the way it is." She smelled the alcohol on his breath as he walked away; his brilliantine was so strong that even in the smoke-filled air it left a distinct odor. The stout saxophonist, with the characteristically puffy face of musicians who have played for many years in night clubs, was clumsily imitating American soloists. A drunken woman laughed hysterically, clinging tightly to her partner; her hands spread as though webbed, very white, with plump fingers. Agnieszka smiled bitterly. The dance ended abruptly and dozens of sweaty-faced dancers went by her on their way back to their seats. A drunk lingering on the dance floor cried, "More!" Two women dragged him to a table. Lights were turned up; the musicians wiped their foreheads and put down their instruments.

"You look like the Mona Lisa," someone said to Agnieszka from behind her. "Do you have such a sad face because, like her, you have no pretty Tissot wrist watch? We might have a talk on that subject . . ."

She went on into the bar. There was a dreadful crowd; people were screaming, singing, abusing one another, clinking glasses, and exchanging kisses and handclasps. Behind the counter two barmen in white aprons ran back and forth. One was small and thin, with a mobile, cheerful face; the other was tall, and his face was impenetrably calm. He wielded his glasses with stony seriousness; in serving each customer he acted like a surgeon preparing for an operation, convinced, however, that everything would go well, according to the will of his hands and brain. He did not react at all to the desperate cries of the drinkers, working according to his own, extraordinarily precise plan.

Finally she made her way to Grzegorz. He sat at the far end of the counter, where the nickel ended in a gentle curve. He looked straight ahead of him with bleary eyes, not speaking to anyone. There was a striking resemblance; like her, he was tall, with hair that could not be called definitely either dark or light; his eyes, like hers, changed color with the weather, ranging from light blue to dark green. His face was puffy, and he had a short nose; lines around his mouth pulled it downward. He leaned his head on his hand. When Agnieszka touched it, he started.

"Did she come?" he asked.

She shook her head. "No," she said. "You're really soaking it up, Grzegorz."

He looked at her with an empty glance as at an inanimate object. "It's not impossible that you're right," he said. He pulled a glass of water nearer him. "But what inference do you draw from this?"

"I feel like having a couple of drinks with you," she said. "And I don't want to have to do with a dead man, like the day before yesterday. Can you buy me a drink?"

"I don't know whether I can," he said, "but I will." He beckoned to the barman. "Fill 'em up," he said in a confidential whisper. He lifted his glass and clinked it with Agnieszka's. They drank. He looked at her unseeingly. "So she didn't come, after all," he said. His voice sounded sober; Agnieszka realized that he was trying to get drunk but couldn't.

"No," she said, "she didn't come."

He smiled. "I know that without your telling me," he said. "Do you by chance know why the devil I'm asking?"

"I know. But she didn't come."

He nodded. The cheerful barman asked: "Another round?" Without waiting for an answer, he quickly filled their glasses and vanished among the bottles.

The orchestra struck up again; drinkers got down off their bar stools, and began to elbow their way toward the dance floor.

"I knew she wouldn't come," said Grzegorz. "The nights are the worst, Agnieszka. I close my eyes and see her; she holds out her hands and says something to me that I can't hear or understand. It seems to me that in her home she also stares into the darkness and addresses her prayers to me just as I address my prayers to her. But when I open my eyes I see only a corner of Zawadzki's bed, and a piece of the ceiling. I hear the faucet dripping. Couldn't that faucet be repaired? And then I lie awake for hours. When a taxi stops in front of the house, I get up from bed and walk over to the window. It seems to me that she will get out of the taxi, come up for me, and that all this torment will end. I count the steps on the staircase, the shadows and the voices. Will you fix that faucet tomorrow?"

"Yes."

He fell silent. He pushed their glasses over toward the barman. "Fill them up, please," he said. "And some kind of water. . . ."

"Hasn't he had enough?" The barman looked questioningly at Agnieszka.

She shook her head. "Please, fill them up," she said.

He filled the glasses and walked away. Two elderly men drank to each other. "Here's to you. My name's Wacek, and yours?" "Jozek." "Which Jozek? Pilsudski?" "No." "The other one?" "Neither. Jozio Kwiatkowski." "Well, here's how." "Here's how." The orchestra was playing a tango. Agnieszka lifted a corner of the curtain separating the bar from the dance floor and watched the dancers. A small man standing beside her said: "I'm getting out of this country. Here you can only be a drunk or a hero. Normal people have nothing to do here. So long." He paid and walked away.

"Is today Thursday?" Grzegorz asked.

"By now it's Friday."

"Till Sunday," he said. "If only I can stick it out till Sunday. Then everything will be clear: either— or. That's what she said: she needed one week to think it over. Only two or three days to go. If she doesn't come before Sunday evening, this means the end. And then . . ."

"What then?" she asked sharply.

He raised his head and looked her straight in the eyes. He was silent for a while. "Then nothing," he said. "I'll go on living. That's the worst of it."

"It's not the worst when you're twenty-five," Agnieszka said.

He shrugged his shoulders. "What does it prove?" he said with an air of contempt. "Moreover, who is twenty-five today? And what of it? How can this knowledge help me? I hope you won't be so stupid as to tell me that I have my life before me, that everything is still ahead of me, and so on. There's not a man alive who really believes that. Every human feeling is sacred and there is no guarantee that a man will want to be foolish for the second time in his life and give another woman as much as before, and after all that's what's in question. 'To give everything.' After all, that's what you call all those douches, rubber caps, and abortions, don't you?"

"Well, what then?"

"I think Slowacki has one of his characters ask, Is the soul a lamp that never burns out? Before every good human feeling we should kneel as before a shrine, as before a star. We should protect it, carry it like a light, and if there is even a little spark left, blow till we're out of breath. This is the Twentieth Century, Agnieszka: Isolde lives in a brothel, and Tristan gets drunk with the pimps at the corner bar. People today have little time for great feelings; they hop out of bed early, lap up their little soup in milk bars, squeeze into streetcars, quarrel with conductors over pennies, buy flimsy furniture in department stores on the installment plan, and so on. To kneel," he said, "to kneel. Life gives no guarantees regarding the future. Everyone who says, 'Give it up, in a few years something else will come along,' deserves to be spat in the face. What will come? When will it come? Every bit of happiness comes the bad way."

He paused and nodded to the barman. He looked into the filled glasses after the barman had gone. A woman sitting a few stools farther along sang in a squeaky voice, "I am so tiny . . ." "But you can hold a lot," said a male voice with conviction. The woman stopped singing; she bent over her glass, mumbling something unintelligible. The saxophonist was still trying to imitate American jazz. The cheerful barman cast an alert glance at Grzegorz. "Coffee?" he said.

Grzegorz came to. "If you say so," he said, "but it's a waste of effort; today I won't get drunk anyway." He turned to Agnieszka: "Want some coffee?" She nodded. "Two coffees, please," Grzegorz said. The barman came back and put two cups before them. Grzegorz tasted his and shook his head sadly. "The coffee is lousy, too," he said.

The cheerful barman spread his hands. "It's the times we live in," he said, and walked away.

"To hell with the times," said Grzegorz. "Another

idiotic myth." He turned to Agnieszka. "Something occurred to me."

"Yes?"

"I'd like to write something some day."

"A book?"

"Yes, a book."

"About love?"

He burst out laughing, and the lines around his eyes turned white. "Oh, no," he said. "To write about love is to make yourself ridiculous. So far, at least, all love literature is nothing but glorified crap. God, what has it got to do with love? I'd like to read something about myself and my feelings when for the twentieth night in a row I can't sleep and lie staring at the ceiling. Everything written on the subject is insipid, like brass compared with the sun. Only Dostoevsky is a little bit truthful, but you run away from his love with your hands burned, like from a red-hot iron. This isn't for modern man. Not for the times we live in." He bent toward Agnieszka and took her hand. "Listen," he said, "this will be something entirely new. The story of two people. We won't call them by their right names nor will we invent names for them." He was slightly drunk all the same, and his speech got a bit thick; his breath was searing. He said: "Yes, this is something entirely new. The story of two people who met at one of life's bad corners. I don't know yet who they are, I have to make up my mind, see? He must be commonplace, very commonplace; she too, probably, though I don't know. . . . Let's say, he drinks too much and complains, could be, no? What else was there to do during that time, except drink and grumble? In Poland drunks have a privileged status, drunkenness has become something like a new special morality. It's known that when a man drinks, something's eating him. But never mind, let's get back to our subject. . . . And what about her? Devil knows what kind of person she ought to be. She must have been through a great deal, she must somehow be resigned or embittered. Whenever anything starts up, it's hard to believe that this time it really will be worth while. This customer, for instance, is out to get drunk, because he's in a hurry to destroy something in himself, he's afraid of suffering, and so on. She's running away from all that too, for to tell the truth her friend is no good, he drinks like a fish, brawls, has a stretch of bad life behind him. And yet there is something good in him, somehow, somewhere. At some point, on the seventh day, there must be something worth while, something good, and they want somehow to dig through to it, at any price. The earth is a lousy place, life is a comical little hell, but somewhere deep underneath the surface, molten metal glows white hot. And they try to build up that worthwhile thing by sheer will power. It falls apart a thousand times each day, each hour, but they start it all over again a thousand times. Perhaps everything might even turn out well in the end, who can tell? But then people begin to help them."

He suddenly straightened himself and pushed Agnieszka's hand away. "People," he said. "Goddam stupid people who never have enough of their own little hell and stick their noses into other people's hells. They begin to touch it all with their sweaty hands, to whisper, to plan, to help, to draw them aside, and to inform them about themselves. 'Do you know,' they tell him, 'that she lived with this man and that man?' 'Do you know,' they say to her, 'that in 1947 he murdered the stationmaster at Mysliborz, as well as the cashier and the assistant engineer? Do you know that he's this and she's that?' People meddle, people lie, people invent ignoble nonsense, and then one day nobody knows what's true and what's a lie, what is slander and what is reality, who is a friend and who is a pig, who is a buddy and who is a bum; there's just no way of knowing what's what, and they decide to part. . . ."

He stopped; his jaw muscles trembled. Now he

looked pitiful. The cheerful barman glanced at him and asked: "Fill it up?"

He nodded, then took his glass and drank it down in one gulp. Agnieszka asked: "Is that the end?"

"Not at all," he said without looking at her. "That would be too simple, and after all people want to understand each other to the bitter end. But I don't know what is to come next. It's the end, obviously it's the end, but something else has to happen first. Yes, yes, I'm sure of that, but I still don't know exactly what . . . Something extraordinarily banal. This doesn't have to be a good book, why the devil should it be good? Anyway, no one will write a book about true love, such things are too terrible and too ridiculous, no one dares reveal them completely. . . . What will it be then? What's needed is something banal, something stinkingly banal. Perhaps illness? Or some sort of moon, some moonlit water? Some such thing must exist, after all; you think about it too. A railroad accident, a disaster, death? Death, perhaps death? When all's said and done, nothing can be more banal. And so, what kind of death, Agnieszka? Caused by the bite of a poisonous ant, by a brick dropping from a scaffolding? Perhaps suicide? But who—he or she? No, he, obviously, despite everything, women love life more than men. Yes. Now I have it."

He paused for breath. His hair clung to his forehead, he pushed it back. His face was sweaty and swollen, his eyes had grown smaller.

"He kills himself," Agnieszka said. "And that's the end?"

He pondered a while. "No," he said, "despite everything, it isn't the end yet. It's barely the first half, the end is still far away. The suicide doesn't come off, Agnieszka, in this story nothing can be successful. What comes later is even worse, because it turns out that the things we're scared of and blackmailed by here on earth amount to very little. But what comes later? Happy endings are never too clever in literature. They part. The end. Period. Maybe they'll try to live intelligently, maybe they won't, who can tell? But at this point we must put an end to it, the game is up. So they part. The pursuit of happiness is over and done with. It's always pointless, but it is worth while to sacrifice one's life for it. This isn't me, it's Stendhal. Is it worth it or isn't it?" he asked the barman.

"It is," said the barman.

"It isn't," said Grzegorz, "but never mind. Two more vodkas, please."

"She wouldn't forgive you that," said Agnieszka.
"What?"

"What you've just said."

"She won't come anyway."

"Do you want to destroy everything?"

"Yes," said Grzegorz. "I don't want to remember anything. It's too cruel to ask a man to recall his most sacred moments. Memories are garbage."

"What's the title of this book?" Agnieszka asked.

"Hard to tell," he said hesitantly. "Anyway it will live only in my imagination. After all, I'm a chemist, goddam it. As for the title—something about silence, about the need to be silent in front of others. So what should it be?"

The bar had been emptying. The cheerful barman busied himself wiping the counter with an immense rag. The espresso machine had stopped hissing, the orchestra had long been silent. Someone was asleep, his head on his arms. A friend tugged at him, saying over and over again: "Bolek, stand up . . . Bolek, don't be drunk . . . Bolek, don't be a pain in the neck. . . ."

"We're closing now," the cheerful barman said. "Till tomorrow."

Grzegorz paid, and they walked out together. A chilly wind was sweeping the streets. Grzegorz bent toward Agnieszka and took her hand; his was sweaty and hot.

"Will she come?"

"The lovers met too late," Agnieszka said. She yawned, she felt sleepy.

Grzegorz burst out laughing. "Agnieszka, that's another fairy tale," he said, letting go of her hand. "I'm only a little older than you, but I can tell you this: I've never yet seen people who met at the right moment in life. There is no such moment in life, and there can't be. It always seems too late or too early, there is too much experience or too little. There is always something that stands in the way. This can't be important." After a moment he asked: "Did you like it?"

"No, I hate sadness. Silence and black colors— they're only good for the dead."

"I won't drink any more, Agnieszka," Grzegorz said. "It seems to me that I love you very much. I wish you were at least a bit different."

They stopped. The night sky was thinning out; it was dirty and full of empty clouds. The dawn clung to the damp roofs. Taxi drivers yawned, the first milk carts dragged along; someone was following them from a distance, cursing at the top of his lungs.

"I too love you very much," said Agnieszka. "You know yourself how much."

4

The leaves were thick and covered the sky; lying flat on their backs they saw nothing overhead except a mass of greenery; nor could they see the singing birds. The warm grass had a bitter smell, and at ground level a low wind brought the scent of pine and the first heather. Now and then squirrels darted out of the thick undergrowth; they stared attentively with their beady little eyes, and after a while scrambled up into the branches with unbelievable speed.

"That's all I remember of my childhood."

"A squirrel?"

"Yes. We once had a squirrel at home. It was given me when I was ten."

"What did you call it?"

"Joasia. It wasn't afraid at all. I slept with it, it ran after me like a puppy, and when I ate, it stuck its nose in my plate."

"And then?"

"Joasia died. Squirrels' teeth grow too long unless they eat nuts. One day it couldn't open its mouth, and there was nothing we could do about it."

"Why didn't you give it nuts?"

"That was under the occupation. Mainly we ate bread with jam. As far as I know, the jam then was made of beets."

"Is that really all?"

"What do you mean, all?"

"Is that all you remember?"

"Isn't it enough for you? Why remember everything?"

"Tell me."

He shrugged his shoulders. "The other things I'd rather not remember."

"Are there a lot of them?"

"Enough."

"That's strange."

"What's strange?"

"We know so little about each other."

"Little?"

"Terribly. Every day you're different."

"But you don't want my memories. Every time I begin to talk you ask me to stop."

"I want different ones."

"But those are the most important."

"I want you to forget those. That's the first thing I'd like to do for you. Don't remember those things, Pietrek."

"So what is it you do want to know about me?"

"For instance, what are you thinking right now?"

"And if it's silly?"

"Let it be. After all, one doesn't go to Bielany with Einstein. Talk."

He put his arms around his knees. She raised his face: he had a pure profile, calm in its youthful severity.

"I'm thinking of when this torment will end, these meetings in cafés, parks, movie theaters. . . ." He closed his eyes, and a painful grimace formed around his mouth. "Walls," he said, "four walls, Agnieszka. To be with you for a week; a day and a night together, then I could die. This is terrible: each day I spend without you is stolen from my life. How many such days have there been? How many will there be? First those years, and now this wandering. . . . No one will give them back to us, no day can return. How many good days could we have had behind us? How long will it go on like this?"

"Don't talk about it, Pietrek."

"Sometimes I don't want to believe all that," he said. "We're alone, completely alone, do you understand? And no one will help us, no matter how much we beg and no matter whom we ask. I suppose there's no one anywhere who can give us a wall. We must wait—and that's that. We must wait and wait, a very long time, and if in the end we get what we want, we probably won't have the strength to enjoy it. We'll have lost many days of our lives unnecessarily. That's the worst."

"Many people have no walls."

"Many people have nothing at all. But that's no reason."

"That's life."

"I don't like that phrase. What does it mean, after all?"

"Everything."

"And nothing."

"Maybe. Now it's summer. You should go some place, Pietrek. To rest up."

"And when I'm back everything will start all over ·again. We'll long for each other, and kiss in doorways after sunset. Then we won't sleep for nights on end, and we'll think about how we can be helped and by whom. And we'll be parting continually. We'll long for each other, torment each other, quarrel, and abuse each other. Not because we're not in love. No. Just because we have no walls. If Romeo and Juliet lived in Warsaw in the year 1956 they would probably never meet. And the worst of it is, it's nobody's fault."

He fell silent. He stared up at the green dome of the trees, and after a moment said: "The worst of it is I love you. With others all this would have been so easy."

"What?"

"Everything and nothing."

He lay flat on his back, his arms under his head. Through the thick foliage he gazed at the red sun setting. It did not take long: the woods began to grow dark, and the leaves lost their color. Nearby was a rifle range, and the soldiers who had finished their day were coming back, singing, "The night is so long." They drew out the last syllable, finishing it abruptly. "Three, four," a voice roared, and they sang in chorus: "It's a pity to waste it." A sleepy breeze came from the warmed river.

"Peter."

"Yes."

"Have you got that room?"

"Yes."

"Tomorrow?"

"Yes."

"He won't be there?"

"We'll be alone."

"You didn't tell him that you'd come with me?"

"No."

"What am I to say at home?"

"Best don't say anything."

"I must. Mother'd be nervous."

"Say that you're going out of town."

"Where?"

"Any place."

"What for?"

"Anything."

"Think of something."

"To Podkowa Lesna. To visit a friend. To study together for the exam. Why do you talk like that? How old are you, Agnieszka?"

"When I'm with you, I'm twenty-two. And you?"

"A hundred."

"Why do you say that?"

47

"Does the date on my birth certificate matter? There are places on earth where every day is a century. One only has to get there."

"What year were you arrested?"

"Fifty-two."

"It won't happen again, will it?"

"If all that were to happen again, if all that had to be repeated, no one would survive. . . . When I was there I thought about you, do you know?"

"Where?"

"At Mokotow."

"You didn't know me then."

"That's unimportant. I thought that if I got out I'd meet you. And that we'd never part, and that I'd never return there. I died every day at sunrise, and every day I came back to life. The commander there was some colonel. He would say to us: 'This is Mokotow. People who get out of here push up the daisies.' At interrogations he screamed: 'We'll kill you the Bolshevik way, a bullet in the back of the head. . . .'" Then I thought about you."

"What has become of him now?"

"The commandant?"

"Yes."

"He's been arrested. I read about it somewhere."

"Does it make you happy?"

48

"Too late to make me happy."

"You won't think about it ever again, right?"

"If I didn't have you, I'd think about it all the time. Now I think you are the person given me by fate as a reward, to make up for the bad old days. Only you. But it's hard to forget, I tell you, Agnieszka. There are things one probably can't ever forget. I remember once . . ."

"Now things will be different, won't they?"

"Why do you say that all the time?"

"I must."

"Well, then things must be different."

"When we have a place we won't let anyone inside for a year. We'll have a sign on the door, saying, 'No one at home. Gone away for a year.' "

"That's funny."

"Why?"

"I once was in a cell with a man who dreamed the same thing. 'After I finally get out of this charming little place,' he would say, 'I'll lock myself up at home and won't stick my nose outside. To hell with all that cherished freedom.' It seems dreams are the same on both sides of the bars."

"What kind of furniture will we have?"

"At times no one could fall asleep," Piotr said, and she knew at once that now he would not listen to any of the things she wanted to tell him, and that she would have to listen to him, although she knew every one of his recollections of that place. Piotr said: "We talked in whispers. We told each other everything—delusions and facts alike. No one knew why or what for, and no one listened anyway. Everyone unreeled his own film in his own head. Each of us thought only of himself, and of his own affairs which didn't exist . . ."

"Stop talking about all that," she said. "Think of our home. And your son. We are going to name him Fyodor, aren't we, after Dostoevsky . . . ?"

"I recalled everything, my whole life, every single last thing that happened. I recalled every person I had ever spoken with, all the words that were spoken, every single day, every single night; finally I reached the point of trying to recall every single thought. What I thought one year, five years, ten years before. What had I done? At what moment in my life had I made the fatal blunder, the thing about which I knew nothing, about which no one would tell me anything? Had one of my friends been a spy? Had someone worked for the political police? Who was the man responsible for putting me where I now found myself? What did he look like? Was he old or young? Did he live alone or did he have a family? Where had I met him? At a bar, at school, in the street, in the sports stadium? How had it begun? And what had I talked to him about? Sometimes I would hang on in my thoughts to someone, a person who suddenly seemed must be the man I was looking for. And then I would think: it is he, it can't be anyone else, it must be he. What had I done to him? What had he done? How had he managed to get me here? Had he done it on purpose, or had I been caught with him? I choked with hatred for him, and then somebody else would occur to me, and all over again I would try to remember where I had met him, and what he had looked like, and what I had talked to him about, and what he could have reported about me."

"Don't think about it," said Agnieszka. "Don't talk about it, think what tomorrow will be like. There will be no one except us. You'll snuggle up to me. I'll hug you, and you'll stop thinking about it. You'll stop thinking about an apartment, and about the prison, and about everything that torments you. The only important thing will be us, and our few hours before daybreak. Yes?"

"Yes, Agnieszka. But who was he? Will I never know?"

"Try to think that you won't. What do you need him for? Do you want to take revenge on him?"

"No, no . . . I'd just like to look at him, if only for a second. To look at his face for one second. Nothing more. I think that if I could see him once, I'd understand many things about my life. Perhaps even everything. That's what I think sometimes. And I suppose I'd give everything for it."

"Even me?"

"Even you."

"In that case it's a good thing that you'll never know anything about it. Now we must go."

"So soon?"

"I want to do some studying tonight . . ."

"Agnieszka."

"What, darling?"

"If I didn't have you, I wouldn't want to live. You are now the only thing I really believe in. You, nothing else. I suppose I have the right to think so. If I didn't have you, I'd do everything to go to pieces completely, to destroy myself, so as never to love, never to believe, and never to suffer again. Without you this side of the prison bars has no meaning for me, it would be just like the other side. Do you understand?"

"Yes. But stop talking about it. Think of tomorrow."

"All right."

"Promise me. Promise that you'll think only of tomorrow, that you won't even mention the other thing. All right?"

"Yes."

"Will you take me home?"

"Why do you ask?"

They rose and walked in the direction of the streetcar. The woods were quiet, grown enormous in the dusk. The domes of the trees merged into each other and into the dark sky.

5

Brzeska Street was not yet asleep. This was the fifteenth of the month, and as always on payday, men were standing around in front of their houses. Their shirts were unbuttoned; their chests, hair, and faces glistened with sweat. Before the day had gone, its leaden sky had harassed houses, bodies, pavements, and trees. There were those who stood and those who sat; those who walked from one end of their street to the other, from one little group to the next, from one street lamp to the next; those who lounged against the walls on patches of trampled grass; those whose disheveled heads leaned out from dirty ground floor windows—all were drinking: beer, vodka, and cheap wine straight from the bottle; they choked as they drank, and the liquor splashed over the sores on their hands, onto their sweaty shirts, and their soft relaxed bodies. The wind, like a tired animal, ran clumsily along the sidewalks, bearing the smell of their sweat, their tobacco, and their breath, hot and rancid with alcohol. Among them women glided to and fro, some in old dressing gowns or with overcoats hastily thrown over their slips, others wearing brightly colored dresses with dark half-circles of sweat under the arms; some were urging the men to come back home; others to go into town for further reveling. They quarreled with the men, drew them away from their comrades, snatched bottles out of their unwilling hands; and they reviled the men in the men's own coarse language.

Agnieszka was familiar with paydays; she knew what Saturday, Sunday, and the nights before holidays were like in this street. Each time she turned into the great buzz that filled that street from wall to peeling wall, she was overcome with fear—a stifling, heavy, and repulsively intimate fear, for she had lived with it for many years. She tried to pass by quickly, defending herself against the drunks, and pushing back the men on the make whenever she did not manage to avoid them altogether. Today she hoped she could safely run the gantlet of all those bleary eyes.

55

She pressed close to Piotr and shut her eyes. They entered the street with their arms about each other. It was only a few hundred yards to the house where she lived, and at first she thought they would pass unnoticed. Then, from a doorway where several of them stood—their faces could not be seen in the dark —someone said to Piotr: "Look out for that tail, it's loaded."

Piotr started forward. Agnieszka held him back with all her weight. "Don't! I beg you, don't!"

"Let go of me!"

"They'll kill you!"

She sank her nails into the palm of his hand, and with each step sank them deeper, so that she felt the pulsation of his veins. She whispered: "If you make a move, I won't go with you, I won't, I won't."

They walked on. Someone said: "Why did they annoy her? I know her."

"Is she a good girl?"

"I'm sure of it."

"Leave her alone, you bully."

"Hoodlum, you mean. A hoodlum always has it ready."

"Baby doll!"

"Come on, just once, you could make me very happy."

56

"Hello, girlie."

"Don't be so stuck up."

"Looks like a real geisha."

"Ever tried her?"

"Me? Such things aren't for me. I'm a modest man."

"Where can you find the strength for it? Not on potatoes."

"Don't worry. If she gave it to you, you'd do it six times."

"In six months maybe."

"Don't," Agnieszka whispered, "please, don't."

"Do you live alone, lady?"

"I'd try her, but he won't take his hands off it."

"A sturdy girl, Zfyszko. She'd kill you."

"Christ, if she'd only let me!"

"Ask her, maybe she's generous."

"She can't say no."

"From a doll like that Michalowski caught the whole works."

"Syphilis?"

"Siberian chancre."

"Don't," whispered Agnieszka, "don't . . ."

"Very pretty!"

"God! One shot at it, and I'd die happy."

"I'd work at it all night."

57

"Hot stuff."

"What of it?"

"Don't get upset. There's a way for a sparrow to satisfy a mare."

"Don't put your head down."

"I can lift my head all right. But who'll lift that thing?"

"Does this little squirt actually screw her?"

"He must jump like a rabbit at it, busy as a barber."

"Can he make her come? He's so puny!"

"Ask him."

"Hey fella, how do you do it?"

"Here, let me lend you mine!"

"Never do that. Once I loaned mine to a friend for his wedding, and look what he gave me back."

"I'm looking. I don't see anything."

"That's the point."

"Ask her how much she wants."

"How much do you have?"

"Twenty zlotys."

"You know what you can do with twenty zlotys."

They turned into the doorway. It was dark, and they blessed the darkness. The street was silent now, and they could hear only their own feverish breathing. Agnieszka leaned heavily against the wall, they had to catch their breath. Her face stood out against the wall, a pale spot. He saw the terrible look in her eyes. There was a smell of urine and of laundry, coming from one of the upper floors. A truck rumbled by, cats were serenading each other. Pietrek said hoarsely: "Nothing happened, nothing. There was only the woods, there is only tomorrow. Do you hear me?"

He tried to take her hand, but she wrested herself free. She was silent and he again could only hear her rapid breathing. In the janitor's room the radio sang hoarsely: "I shall walk along a silvery path among the gardens . . ." Someone abruptly turned it off; and once again there was only silence punctuated by the cats screaming.

"Nothing happened," Piotr repeated. "Tomorrow at this time we'll be together, tomorrow at this hour . . ."

He stretched out his hands toward her head. Then, with all her strength she struck his face with her fist. He reeled, stumbled against a box lying on the ground, and fell. His head hitting the concrete gave a hard sound.

"Go away," she cried. "Go away, go!"

Without looking back, quickly, taking three steps at a time, she ran upstairs.

6

Once in the flat, she hung up her overcoat and went into the living room, almost unconscious, shaking all over. Her father was walking on his hands. His shirt had slid out of his trousers. His face was swollen from the effort, his eyes were bloodshot; he breathed heavily, drops of sweat rolled down his bald pate; the spectacle was repulsive, and Agnieszka averted her eyes. This mania of her father's she found particularly revolting, although she pitied him a little. When he saw her, he performed an adroit somersault, and stood up in front of her, beaming with satisfaction.

"I've still got some strength, hm?" he asked.

"Probably a good deal."

"You young people have no idea," he said, "what a

splendid thing physical strength is. Sometimes, looking at those weaklings, I feel sorry for them: today's men are as feeble as stewed spiders." He took his upper plate out of the glass and put it smartly into place. He was still flexing his muscles: they looked hard and round, running like little mice under his faded skin. He lighted a cigarette, stuck it in a wooden holder, and asked: "I don't think they'll fire me just yet, will they?"

She shrugged her shoulders. "Where do you get such ideas?"

He smiled sadly. "You're laughing," he said, "but that's not funny at all. They're quick these days to fire older men, and it isn't easy to find a job. Recently I had to deal with one such elderly man who had been embezzling money for several years, trying to put something away for his old age. Somehow he managed to get away with it, and was declared irresponsible. There are many such cases."

He stopped talking and stared at his hands. Suddenly he looked into her face. "Agnieszka," he said, and she sensed alarm in his words, "do I look my fifty-five years?"

He moved his face closer to hers, and she felt his unhealthy, sour breath. He looked far older; he was creased, bald, his skin was flecked with liver spots, and there were heavy bags under his eyes. He was ruined, what is called ruined, by the war, by discomfort, by poor food: his muscular body strong as an animal's contrasted with his aged face. She gazed at him for a time—he reminded her of a poor old dog; she could think of no other comparison. She averted her eyes, and burst out laughing.

"You look forty-five at the most," she said. "I think that, generally speaking, you have nothing to worry about. Many men would envy you your strength."

He breathed with relief. "You should practice gymnastics," he said. "It helps a great deal." Then, suddenly changing his tone: "Where is Grzegorz?" he asked.

"I don't know," she said. "I've just come back. Has no one come to see Grzegorz?"

"No. Do you have any idea where he might be?"

The mother, who had remained silent until then, spoke: "Why ask her? She doesn't care about what goes on at home. She has to run around with her boy friend, that's the most important thing to her. You could die, I could die, but she must let herself go with him."

"Do you want me to let myself go with you?" Agnieszka asked.

The mother sat up; for a moment they stared at

each other. Then the mother closed her eyes, and her face took on her usual martyred expression. Agnieszka banged the door and walked out to the kitchen. Without turning the light on she put the tea kettle on the gas range. Only now, lifting the heavy kettle of water, did she feel a pain in her hand; she held it up to her eyes, and examined it in the light of the street lamp—her knuckles were bruised. She gazed at the hissing blue flame, thinking: "Tomorrow you won't come. Tomorrow the key will be under the mat, as you have agreed with Roman, and no one will pick it up. If there were a thought-reading machine, you'd know what is happening to me. I doubt if I can ever tell you myself. People can't understand each other in these matters. In what matters can people understand each other? When it comes to borrowing ten zlotys, a pair of shoes, or a wringer. That's the limit of our possibilities. Someone said once that darkness separates man from man; we once heard it said, both of us. And here's a gas flame. It gives a bit of light, a bit of warmth. We can make tea. Or cook oatmeal for breakfast. But we can do more. We can throw out this kettle, lock the door, snuff out the flame, and try not to think of anything. Not to think that father is gradually turning into an ape, that in a moment I must go back in to them and

go to bed, and that we surely won't meet tomorrow . . ."

Her father came in. "Mother wants her camomile
tea," he said. He walked over to the light switch and
put out his hand.

"Don't turn on the light," Agnieszka said. Her face
was still wet.

He stopped. "Are you dreaming?"

"Yes."

He sat down; as usual he clasped his hands on his
knees. He bent forward to her from the waist. "I'd
like to know what about," he said, trying to sound
jolly.

"A fairy-tale prince."

"Has he a palace?"

"Not for the present, but for several years he lived
in a palace."

"Was it built of crystal?"

"Yes. And concrete and steel."

"What did he see from his window?"

"That depends. I suppose not much. They put iron
shutters of some kind over the windows, to discourage you from running away. There was probably
a humanistic intention behind it, but if anyone sings
you a song about a prisoner who gazes at the blue

sky from behind his bars, you have the right not to believe it. In fact, nothing can be seen."

"What are you talking about, Agnieszka?"

"It's all right," she said. "Everything is all right. You look forty-five, and next year we'll increase production of tires for tractors by 15 per cent. In the end Zawadzki will move out of here, and our sky is not empty: a few weeks ago there were pictures of Polish jets in all the newspapers. We'll also export Polish automobiles to Pakistan, and the number of miners who are amateur beekeepers will increase fourfold. Everything is all right," she cried, "only don't ask me to tell you what I think about and how I think!"

He rose and came over to her. "Mother has irritated you," he said in a low voice. He put his hand on her shoulder. "You must be indulgent toward her. Remember, she has been bedridden for several months, and no hospital wants to admit her. You know that the hospitals are overcrowded. You must be indulgent."

"Mother is incurably ill," said Agnieszka. "The doctors know it better than you. They won't admit her because they have to save others. She will die here."

He loosened his grip and sat down heavily. She saw

that he was staring at her face, and she drew back further into the darkness.

"In the end they'll admit her," he said after a while.

"No," said Agnieszka. "We must have no illusions. Under the circumstances, while there is no room for others, they shouldn't admit her. She must stay with us."

"Don't you love Mother?"

She shrugged her shoulders. "Her fate concerns me," she said.

He passed his hand over his forehead. He had suddenly begun to stoop, and was now merely a pitiful old man, his strong muscles notwithstanding.

"I often think about it," he said. "This would probably be best for her. Why should she suffer unnecessarily in this house, with me, with you, with those drunks in the street? The end is always the end. We must understand that moment, when everything is behind us. Old age is creeping up on me, too. There should be houses where old men could be done away with painlessly. When I am no good for anything, I'll ask Grzegorz to give me some sleeping pills. Maybe his chemistry will be useful, after all."

"Then why worry?" Agnieszka said. "You'll meet Mother in heaven, and there you'll continue your wonderful life together. And now, enough of this nonsense. Turn on the light, we'll make the camomile tea."

There was singing in the street. She closed the window with a bang. She walked over to the stove, and staring at a lid of a saucepan, she thought: "Where are you going now? What are you feeling, what are you thinking? How can one find one's way in this tangle of drunkenness, concrete, insane ravings, and foolishness? If I could only know what you look like just now? Will we meet tomorrow? And if we do, what will we say to each other to begin with? 'I'm sorry'—no. 'I was carried away'—no. 'I don't know why I acted like that'—no. Do you know what? Let's agree not to say anything. We'll never say a word on this subject. We'll go straight for the key; we'll open the door and we'll find ourselves at last within four walls, no one will be there, no bad memories, and everything, everything will be possible . . ."

"It's boiling," her mother called from the living room. "Don't you hear it boiling?"

Agnieszka started, her father too. They exchanged smiles.

"I'll go out for a while," she said. "I've got a headache."

67

"Go see Zawadzki," her father said. "He'll be pleased."

"Is he still tinkering with his motorcycle?"

"Yes."

She smiled again. "Don't worry," she said. "Everything will be all right. Sunday you'll go fishing. That's always something."

He sighed. "Two more days," he said. "I must wait."

"That's nothing. Then you'll feel better."

She threw her coat on, and ran down the stairs. In a corner of the courtyard Zawadzki had built a garage for himself out of rubble, where he kept his motorcycle. She found him bent over the engine.

"Good evening," she said. "Two more horses and you'll be able to go."

"Maybe you should go to bed," he said without raising his head. "Young women shouldn't wander about at night. Might give them foolish ideas."

"Why? I feel like talking with you. How's your fiancée?"

She squatted beside him. He ground his teeth. "If she thinks she's fooling me," he said, "she'll have an unpleasant surprise."

"Better men than you have been deceived by women," Agnieszka said.

68

He suddenly stood up. He lifted the electric bulb attached to a long cable and let the light fall on his face. "Agnieszka," he said dully, "take a good look at me, and tell me whether I look like a man who can be turned into a moron."

Lit up from below, broad-shouldered and tall, with sharp features, he looked formidable. "I've seen you somewhere before," Agnieszka thought suddenly. "No, not you. Someone who looked like you look at this moment. Exactly like you. He even raised his left hand the same way. Where was it and who was it?"

"No," she said, "you don't."

"If all they say is true," he said, "I'll beat her up like the boys in the army beat up a whore who gives them a disease."

"What disease has she given you?"

"I'm afraid that after that it would be hard for me to believe in people," he said. "I have seen a great deal in my life, but I don't want the first woman who comes along to make a complete fool of me." He raised his grease-smeared face to her. "I want to believe in people," he said. "In the end, that is the most important thing of all. Goddam it, can't you understand?"

"Has no girl ever deceived you?"

He laughed unpleasantly. "Nor will any. By God the Father: I was in a concentration camp and I was at the front; sometimes I thought I was in the very center of hell. After all, that teaches you something, don't you think?"

"Of course," she said. She looked at his face again. "Where have I seen such a face," she wondered. "What was it? A man desperately stretching upward —that tense face expressing extraordinary concentration. Where was it? When?" "Devil take you," she said to Zawadzki. "I once saw someone who resembled you terribly. I can't remember when or where. Now I won't sleep all night. Good night, Zawadzki."

She went back into the house. In the hall she ran into her father. He had his overcoat on and was taking his hat from the peg.

"Are you sure Grzegorz didn't say where he was going?" he asked.

"No, he didn't," she said. "All he said was that he wouldn't drink any more."

"Mother can't get to sleep," he said. "She's worried about him. I must find him."

"Go to bed," said Agnieszka. "Why get bawled out if you oversleep tomorrow and are late to the office? I'll look for him myself."

Once again she went downstairs, thinking: "And you, where are you? Did you go out and get drunk, like Grzegorz? And now you're raving; you are buttonholing people, and telling them our story which concerns no one but you and me. Is that what you're doing? Or are you lying somewhere with open eyes and repeating my name, Agnieszka, Agnieszka? Perhaps you're afraid of tomorrow, like me? If at this moment you can understand and guess something, remember: I am with you now. I am with you even if you are lying in the gutter. Even if you've lost your mind and gone to some whore. I am with you everywhere, if only you will think of me."

In the doorway she ran into Zawadzki: he was taking out his motorcycle.

"I'll ride a bit to try it out," he said. "Where are you going?"

"To look for Grzegorz."

"He's drinking?"

"I don't suppose he's down on his knees in some church."

They were now in the street. Zawadzki kicked the starter, and the engine began to throb. "Get on," he said. "I'll give you a lift downtown."

They started noisily. After about a hundred yards,

the engine began to cough. The motorcycle gave a few violent starts, and stopped dead. Agnieszka jumped down from the saddle.

"It's the feedline again," Zawadzki said.

He looked utterly dejected. They stood in the light of a street lamp, and the glow coming from above illumined his sharp features, now immobile. Agnieszka started. "Now I know," she said.

"What?"

"Where I saw a face like yours. Perhaps not a face, but a man standing in the same pose as you now, with the same expression."

"Well?"

"It was in a movie once. A terrorist accidentally kills a man; he must escape, though he is wounded. The whole city is chasing him—the police, stool pigeons, assorted rats; everyone wants to catch him, each group for their own reason. Also his girl is looking for him."

"That's noble of her. And . . . ?"

"In the end she finds him," Agnieszka said. She smiled. "She finds him when he is already dying, and he has no strength left to run. The police are closing in; I remember the searchlights of the police coming closer and closer. The girl decides to die with him. I can even remember the last words of the film. The dying man asks, 'Still a long way to go?' And she answers, 'It's a long way, but we'll walk it together.' "

She stopped.

"And what then?"

"Then they die together, Zawadzki. They're killed by a burst of police bullets. But that isn't the important thing. They believed to the end—that apparently it was necessary, that it was worth while, and not otherwise. Life always holds the threat of separation, but death joins forever."

"You're stupid, do you hear?"

"I hear you. Good night."

She walked away.

7

She looked for him in all the downtown bars, but he was nowhere to be found. She looked into the ones where the elite has its fun, and into the ones where officials bring bottles of vodka in their brief cases and pop the cork under the table. At the Kameralna, Grzegorz's favorite doorman, the mighty Miecio, winked at her and whispered: "He was here, but he took off into town. He's been in love lately, correct?" "Yes," said Agnieszka. By now, after inspecting hundreds of drunken faces and talking to doormen, she was completely exhausted; she was unsteady on her feet, and could only think, "Sleep, sleep. . . ." Miecio took her by the hand and led her to the checkroom; he poured a glass of vodka into her, and said: "Go to the Zieleniak. He went there to get drunk." He put her into a taxicab and slammed the door.

"You want to go there?" the cabby said, surprised, when she gave him the address. He whistled. "It's no place for young ladies."

"How do you know, goddam it," Agnieszka said furiously, "which places are for young ladies?"

He raised his hand and adjusted his mirror to catch the reflection of her; every time they passed a street lamp he slowed deliberately and took a long look. He said nothing for a long time; the taxicab, clanking noisily, dragged itself through the silent city. Finally, he burst out laughing. "You don't look like one," he said. "You really don't." He sighed, then added: "A man's stupid to the end of his life." He put his hand on the meter. "Here you are. Enjoy yourself, you're a big girl now."

She paid the fare and got out of the cab. She walked among standing carts; the horses were asleep, their heads down, noses stuck into their feed bags. Not a single star gleamed in the sky; only the needle above the Stalin Palace glowed, dim and bloody. The immense Zieleniak Square was dark and dead, but she knew that at sunrise it would break into a life of feverish bustle, dubious deals, the rustle of crumpled bills, and hastily exchanged whispers. "Little obscenities are spoken loudly," she thought, deftly stepping over a drunk, "big ones are whispered. As for the truth, one doesn't say it at all. Who can tell whether each truth is not at bottom the greatest obscenity of all?" A horse neighed directly over her head; she jumped aside, swearing aloud.

The place was an enormous barracks; it was much frequented by the teamsters who brought fresh produce into the city. As she came in, she saw him at once. He was sitting near the bar, at a table wet with beer; he was drawing complicated designs with his finger. At the same table a drunk was asleep, his head down. When Agnieszka sat beside him, Grzegorz did not even look up.

"Are you saving mankind?" she said.

"Correct."

"And?"

"The energy of hydrogen bombs. That is the only thing that can fill one with optimism today."

"Very prettily said. Wouldn't you like to come home?"

"She didn't come?"

"No."

"Mother hasn't died yet?"

"No."

"Nothing has changed?"

"No."

Only now did he raise his eyes toward her. "Then what are you here for?" he said.

"I want you to come home."

"You have a sense of humor."

"You know Mother can't sleep when you're out."

"I can't sleep ever. What of it?"

"Grzegorz."

"Well?"

"I've been looking for you half the night."

"Your search has been crowned with success, so why complain?"

"Grzegorz, I'm terribly tired. I want to sleep. Nothing else, just sleep at last. I don't know how many nights now I've been looking for you. Do it for my sake, come home. Drink yourself into a stupor, but do it quickly, and come home."

He looked at her. "You're very pretty," he said. "Your eyes are really green. Your face has a martyred expression. The corners of your mouth are very touching—a kind of childlike helplessness mingled with bitterness. Exiles, and convicts, dream of women like you. That boy friend of yours must be crazy about you, isn't he? Our parents don't like him because he was in prison. That's strange. Whenever I had a girl, our parents liked her. Until the first abortion."

"Let's go home now, Grzegorz."

"Listen to me, Agnieszka. It will be better if you go back alone. I want to go my way to the end. I want to see to what extent a man can stupefy himself. You mustn't watch it. Go and leave me here."

"Do you want to do away with yourself, Grzegorz?"

"Call it what you like. In this case the name doesn't matter. No metaphor hits it off just right. I want to stop loving, suffering, waiting, and believing in things that life doesn't confirm. Do I ask much of my family? All I want is that you forget about me. What right have you to appeal to me in the name of our parents, when you don't love them yourself? Those stupid strangers, full of lies—my only link with them is the address on my identity card—why should we love them?"

She scrutinized him. He was aging; he looked far older than he actually was. Every day the corners of his mouth dropped a little more, the lines around his eyes grew whiter. He might have been handsome were it not for his perpetually swollen face and his glazed, bloodshot eyes, as green as her own. "You idiot," she thought. "If you only knew how truly I love you. Perhaps more than anyone else. If only I could be sure that you actually do stupefy yourself, I wouldn't be sitting here. I know that you say what you really feel. And I, your flesh and blood, your sister, am sitting here, looking at your gloomy face, and I can't do a thing for you; I can't even drag you home. I wish you could realize right now that I really can't do a thing for you."

There was a commotion at the counter. The waiter pulled a man out by the collar; in the doorway one of them gave him a blow with his knee. Agnieszka bent over Grzegorz. "Don't I mean anything to you, either?"

"This is demagogy," he said. "The method is completely discredited. Stalin wasn't successful with it; what makes you think you will be?"

"I don't think. I'm just tired."

"Everybody's tired. There are two things that tie people to each other in Poland—vodka and exhaustion."

"Grzegorz, you know that in the end things will be better."

"I'm sure of it. But tell me, how can we forget what was, how we lived, how people were treated? Party members were rehabilitated after they died, who will rehabilitate me while I'm alive?"

"But you haven't done anything bad."

"I had no power. I had only fanaticism. Within my sphere of action I was a scoundrel. I did my best. This means something too, you know. I swear, it's easier to purge yourself of great errors than of little villainies. I was secretary of my school. I expelled students just because they had an aunt in Pernambuco, or because their great-grandfather had been an informer under the Czars. I tried my hardest, believe me. But now I want to know: just where am I? Am I a swine or a hero? But that's really unimportant: any swine can become a hero if the need for it arises. I want to know what I am to go back to life with. And I want to know for sure that I'll have clean hands in the future."

"You won't learn it here, on the Zieleniak. Moreover, there's still the idea. An idea that is wise and just."

"That's true. But the weak point of each wise idea is that stupid people try to carry it out."

"Those are just words," Agnieszka said. She was so tired she could scarcely keep her eyes open. "You're looking for excuses to drink. You can always find those."

"The very fact that I am alive," said Grzegorz, "is excuse enough for doing anything. But I want to know: What next? You say it's an excuse. All right.

Let me tell you something. Once I ran into an old schoolmate—I hadn't seen him for a few years. We went to a bar and each of us had a couple of drinks. At that time people like him were referred to as 'black reactionaries,' in the official meaning of the term. We talked; we had a real heart-to-heart talk. There were many things I didn't like even then, and he didn't either. Then we went our separate ways. This fellow is an enemy. The worst kind. He has no gun, but he whispers, makes confusion. A man of his sort is more dangerous than an armed gang. In one way or another, his trap has to be shut. And three hours later I met him again—in a security police office. He and I entered the building simultaneously, so it has to be said that history didn't approve of either of us. I defended my faith, my cause before the enemy; he defended his freedom. By God, which of us is a scoundrel, and which a man? To this day I don't know."

He bent toward her. "Even supposing that she'll come," he said, "that she'll come in the end, as the clock ticks off the last minute of Sunday, that she'll leave her husband and her children, and stay with me—what face will I confront her with, what heart? Am I to love her, if I have stopped believing in myself, if I despise myself? Is the world we're living in a place where love can thrive? We don't sleep with women for pleasure any more, but to have something to tell our friends. I don't want my life to be an illusion. I don't want to have to hide my love. And to begin with, I want to know what will become of Poland. What will happen to those who were wronged? To the party? To freedom? I want to know what will happen to those who betrayed my confidence. To those who kept assuring me that I was fighting and winning, when actually I was retreating, acting against the people, losing my faith and my conscience. You can hear your own voice in your throat, but your own life you can perceive only with your conscience. I want to find water to wash my hands in. Does it make sense to talk about love under such circumstances? Everyone has heard that there is such a thing, but—what does it look like? What should it look like? How can we reconcile pure feelings with dirty hands? That's a problem. Not the only one. Today Hamlet with his 'To be or not to be' would be just good enough to serve as errand boy for a small town party secretary. Life has smashed all preconceived patterns like so many clay pigeons: what are we to create to take their place? To be or not to be. People are exhausted, they are dropping on the ground, what can raise them up again? To be or not to be. Cynicism is coming—and fast—to be the sole morality. To be or not to be. Can anything valuable come out of a world that has to use blackmail to keep from collapsing? To be or not to be. Oh, we've created artificial moons, but man with his true feelings and aspirations must find a safe refuge. To be or. . . . Waiter, half a pint, please."

The waiter snatched up the empty bottle as he passed the table. Light—the windows had filled with dirty light. A drunken party entered noisily. Agnieszka quickly took stock of them: all of them were well dressed and gay.

"It's closing time for the night clubs," Grzegorz said. He jerked his head toward the new arrivals. "Architects. They've come here for the last tankful. It's essential to preserve contact with the masses."

The waiter came up, put the bottle on the table. "When will you pay?"

"In a couple of days," Grzegorz said. The waiter walked away. "Look at them," Grzegorz said, "it may make you feel better."

Agnieszka turned her head. There was a throng at the bar, the mood was that of a joyful morning. A tall graying man with noble features, dressed in a magnificently tailored suit of English woolen, was slapping the shoulder of a youngster who looked like an apprentice thief, and talking loudly: "I'm not a stranger, I was a boy just like you. From Wola. Before the war I used to go to the Roxy. I loved cowboy pictures. They played that kind at Wola. Do you know Stasiek Malinowski from Wola?"

"No," the other said, wrinkling his low forehead.

The graying man beamed: "You see, you see. God, those were terrible times. There was hunger, misery. You couldn't even dream of getting a job." He raised his hand in a magnificent sweeping gesture. "Waitress!" he said to the girl behind the counter. "Princess! One round for all. We'll drink to the working class of Wola." He added in Russian: "It's on me." And, turning to the boy: "My name's Andrzej, and yours?"

"Kazik."

"Well, 'attaboy." He handed a glass to the boy. "Here's to you, Kazik. And to Wola!"

Grzegorz rose from his seat. He poured the entire contents of the bottle into a mug, and walked up to the counter. He bowed to a lady in a low-cut gown. "May I join in the toast, gentlemen?" he said.

"Make yourself at home, make yourself at home," several voices said.

"To the working class of Wola," said Grzegorz. He splashed the vodka into the face of the graying man and jumped back. A knife gleamed in the hand of the boy with the low forehead. Grzegorz drew out a gun. He raised his left hand. "Quiet," he said. "Don't move. I won't fight the peasant way. I'll shoot."

They walked out. Outside, Agnieszka said: "Feel better?"

"A little," he said. He put the gun back in his pocket. She gave him a sidewise glance.

"I can't say you lack Polish characteristics."

He shrugged his shoulders, then smiled weakly. "He said himself he liked cowboy pictures," he said. "We must penetrate into the dreams and aspirations of the working class, understand its strivings . . ." He paused. After a while he asked: "Will she come Sunday?"

"I'm sure she will," Agnieszka said, apathetically. She did not believe in herself, in her own words, or in the fading sky.

8

The large hand of the clock was approaching the figure twelve. "It's seven," Agnieszka thought, "he won't come. Surely, he won't come." She felt relieved, and for a moment this drowned out her regret. She was standing under the clock of the Central Station. It was Saturday; people seized with the weekend madness were rushing toward the platform. Loaded with parcels and suitcases, they pushed and cursed each other in the crowd. The loudspeaker blared hoarsely, announcing departing trains; red and green lights went on and off just below it. She looked at the clock again. The hand had passed the number twelve by three minutes. "It's all over," she thought. "So this is what it looks like: lights, noises, and crowds. None of those feelings that others call suffering. Nothing but stupor." The hand jumped another minute; when she lowered her eyes, Piotr was standing before her.

"I couldn't get on a streetcar," he said. "It's Saturday, the big rush. Three times the militia made me get off the step!"

She smiled. "Couldn't they sense that you were going to join me?"

"They don't sense things," he said, "they're the militia. Let's get out of here. I don't like railroad stations. They always remind me of good-bys."

They still had not moved from the spot. They stared at each other. Piotr was pale, his eyes were tired. The loudspeakers blared hoarsely: "The train for Minsk Mazowiecki leaves from. . . ." People rushed by in packs. Agnieszka asked: "Are you angry at me?"

He shook his head. "You can get used to anything," he said.

"Other people did it better than you. They put on thick rubber gloves for the job, the kind miners use. With a glove like that, you can keep punching a man's face for forty-eight hours without leaving a mark. Only the gums swell up a little, like babies' gums when they cut their first teeth. I remember, one night . . ."

"Let's go," said Agnieszka. "What time did he say the key would be there?"

"From six o'clock on. It's there now."

"So what are we waiting for?"

On the way they stopped at a little café. The customers huddled in groups at the round tables, buzzing like flies. A bald fellow sat swaying at an old-fashioned piano made of light-colored walnut; his eyes closed, he banged out a tune with thick fingers. "He's taking a nap, the rascal," Agnieszka thought, and she was surprised to discover that this angered her. After a long while, a stout waitress brought them coffee and cakes; the coffee was almost completely cold, the cakes were repulsive. Piotr was silent; his head down, he was stirring his cup with a spoon unthinkingly.

"You look like a booby," Agnieszka said furiously. She felt a growing anxiety.

"I'm glad of it," he murmured.

"How about saying something?"

"I'm afraid," he said. "I've always been afraid. Nothing's ever come off the way I wanted, and now I'm scared as hell."

Under the table Agnieszka kicked his leg. He winced.

"And what about me?" she said, her voice quivering hysterically. "What am I to say?"

"I suppose you've slept with someone before, no?"

She looked at him with hatred. "Now I'll sleep with you," she growled. "That's the only important thing, isn't it?"

She jumped up suddenly and grabbed him by the hand.

"Let's go."

"The check, for heaven's sake."

"Leave her everything you have, but let's go."

They walked out in a hurry, the coatroom attendant staring after them in surprise. The street ran off into darkness, the twilight irradiated by an occasional street lamp as they walked quietly side by side. He wanted to put his arm around her; she pushed him away.

"What's the matter with you?" he cried.

She stopped. She looked intensely at his face. He had to close his eyes. "Pietrek," she whispered.

"Yes."

"What did you feel when you slept with a woman for the first time?"

"I was sort of happy."

"At being a man at last?"

He laughed drily. "Not at all," he said. "That I'd never be a woman."

"What are we going there for?"

"We can go back."

He saw a moment of hesitation on her face.

"No," she said. "Let's go. I only wanted to know."

Again they walked in silence. When they passed by a street lamp their shadows overlapped, and glided past on one side. Cats were screaming on the roofs. Agnieszka smiled unpleasantly. A cold mass of air blew in from the Vistula, but she felt so warm that she opened the top buttons of her blouse.

"This will be the first time since I was in prison," Piotr said suddenly.

"What?"

"With you."

"Really?" she said unthinkingly.

"Yes. True freedom doesn't come at once."

"Still a long way to go?" she asked after a while.

"Near. A few steps. A hundred yards. Fifty yards. Twenty. Here."

They entered the house. They climbed a staircase. Somewhere higher up an invisible cat was mewing; Agnieszka suddenly longed to murder it. The staircase smelled of laundry, sauerkraut, and fried potatoes, and Agnieszka thought suddenly, "This has happened before. All this happened before somewhere. This staircase, the cat . . ." A man going downstairs glanced at them absent-mindedly; Agnieszka could barely keep from crying out, "Why are you staring like that, you half-wit!" Then they came to a door; before it was the cat they had heard. It spit at them once and ran away. Piotr bent down and reached under the mat. He felt a long time, then stood up. "It isn't there," he stammered. "He hasn't left it."

"Knock," she said sharply.

He hesitated. "Perhaps he couldn't . . ." he began.

She interrupted him: "Knock!"

He knocked gently. No one answered. Agnieszka walked up to the door and kicked it with all her strength; the kitten lurking on the stairs mewed desperately. There was the sound of shuffling steps within, then the key creaked. In the doorway stood a young man with a girlish face. He wore green pajamas; his breath reeked of alcohol.

"Ah, it's you," he stammered at the sight of Piotr. "Damn, how absent-minded I am! The fact is I completely forgot. I'm terribly sorry. Well, never mind, we'll manage somehow. Please, come in."

He stretched out his hand into the dark corridor.

He swayed on his legs a little, but it was clear that he was trying to keep sober. Piotr said, "No, thanks."

"Go in," said Agnieszka. She pushed his back with all her strength. They walked into a long old-fashioned corridor, stumbling against trunks and cupboards. There was a smell of moth balls, and a strange odor of old paper and lavender. The young man in pajamas walked ahead of them, clever in the way he kept steady on his feet.

"Here," he said.

They entered the room. Only a little bulb was glowing. The first thing Agnieszka saw was a completely naked girl sleeping on the cot. When they came in, she did not open her eyes, she did not even start. "Drunk," Agnieszka thought. The young man explained with an embarrassed smile: "I met her on a train. She was going to visit somebody, her husband or fiancé, or whoever." He spread his hands and winked at Agnieszka. "Well, that's that," he said. "It's a small world. In the end everybody meets in bed. But there's another cot. You can do your business, just strip off the cover. We won't disturb each other."

"Thanks, it's very kind of you," Agnieszka said. "We'll do our business in the privy some other time. Is it your kitten that is mewing on the landing?"

"The kitten?" the owner of the flat repeated. "The cat? Yes, it's mine."

Agnieszka turned to Piotr. "Punch him in the jaw. Quick!"

Piotr walked up to the owner of the flat and struck him with his fist in the temple. The young man dropped like a log.

"That's for letting an animal starve," Agnieszka said.

"Let's go," said Piotr.

"Just a minute."

She walked to the switch and turned it. The room grew very bright. Agnieszka squatted near the girl and began to examine her.

"Have you lost your mind?" Piotr hissed. He tugged her hand. "Let's go!"

"I must take a good look at her," she said softly. "Come here. See? She has a pretty mouth, nose . . . it's a pity she's drunk, for we might have seen her eyes. Brown? Blue? Black? It would be interesting to know who is waiting for her. See the nice breasts she has? She can't be more than twenty, I tell you."

"You've gone mad," he said.

"No," she said. She covered the sleeping girl and eased a pillow under her head. "But I'd like to go mad. That would be best."

She rose and walked over to the window. He saw that she was trying to control her tears. He did not go near her. She put her hand on the flowerpot; he saw her white fingers.

The owner of the flat came to. He got up, his eyes were dazed.

"What's this . . . ?" he stammered.

Agnieszka turned about. "Punch him in the jaw, Pietrek," she said quickly.

Piotr swung out. The young man fell again, upsetting a chair.

"That's because you don't water the flowers," Agnieszka said, and smiled at him. "You don't treat either flora or fauna properly. Good night. No hard feelings."

In the street she burst out laughing. He gripped her arm. "What are you doing?" he growled.

They stopped.

"You can't say anything about this situation," she said. "Surely nothing like this happened to you in prison."

He drew back. "It's better we should part," he said. "I'm telling you, Agnieszka, it's better we should part. In every human relationship there is a line one mustn't cross. It's better to give up and save one's memories at least. Respect. Dignity. Despite everything, these things aren't as silly as they may seem."

She smiled again. "So that's all life has taught you? To give up? That prison you're always talking about?"

"Yes," he said. "It's better to give up than to watch everything sink in the mud. I have no desire to die. I must live with something. I must remember something. Something that isn't crap."

"I love you," she said. "And I'll stay with you. I want to go to bed with you today. I don't care where or how."

A party of revelers passed them; they took up the whole width of the sidewalk, reeling gaily. Piotr and Agnieszka moved aside. Piotr said: "Come to my place."

"Your place? But you live with four friends."

"Perhaps they haven't come back yet," he said with despair. "It's Saturday, it's early, perhaps they've gone somewhere. We'll lock ourselves in and won't open for them even if they throw me out tomorrow." He shouted for the whole street to hear: "Come for a moment! At least for a moment!"

They turned back. Again they walked side by side. Silent, they listened to the echo of their own footsteps. They passed bars, stores, movie theaters. Agnieszka looked into lighted windows and thought: "Walls. Four walls. Perhaps three? Can there be a room with only three walls? Could one live in such a room? Is there such a room somewhere?" She tried to think of different things, but one thought dominated all the others—she wanted to sleep, to fall asleep at last. She did not recognize the streets along which Piotr was leading her. She came back to herself only when he had led her through a doorway and they found themselves in a completely dark courtyard. She looked about her in surprise: not a single window was lighted.

"Why is it so dark here?" she asked.

"Don't you see?" He laughed. "These are ruins."

Only now did she notice that the windows were empty. She had not been able to see it at first; the windows barely stood out against the dark sky.

"Is this where you live?"

"We're the only tenants," he said. "We've fixed up this place ourselves. We climb up to our room by a ladder. It's better than a circus. But that's unimportant. They're not in. Do you understand? We're alone, Agnieszka."

"Alone," she repeated. She suddenly put her arms around him, and drew him to her; she began rapturously to kiss his eyes and mouth. "Alone, alone," she stammered. "You understand, you understand?" She pressed herself to him with all her strength. At that very moment a rectangle of light fell on them from above. She closed her eyes. Piotr pushed her away gently.

"They're back," he said. "Only one window is ever lighted here. Mine."

They raised their heads and looked upward. High above them, over the window, the courtyard and the ruins, stars gleamed through the mist. Some animal ran by them, its soft paws thudding on the pavement.

"Tomorrow is Sunday," Agnieszka said hoarsely. "We'll go out of town, do you hear me? We'll take a blanket and go out of town. To the woods, any place. Come for me tomorrow before noon."

She wrenched herself free and ran away; she did not want him to see the tears running down her face. She ran like a madwoman, pushing the passers-by aside. Only after noticing that people were turning to look at her, she stopped running, and began to walk very slowly.

She stood before her house; she had no courage to enter. "Not there again," she thought, "not there again." When she finally made up her mind to go upstairs, she met Zawadzki in the doorway: he was taking out his motorcycle.

"I cleaned the carburetor," he said proudly. "Now it should work. Want to take a ride with me?"

"Thank you very much," she said. "I don't carry life insurance."

"You make up for it by being disagreeable," he said. "If you're interested, your little brother is drinking in the bar three houses away. I saw him there a moment ago. Go get him before he goes any further."

He turned over the motor and drove off. "Go for him?" she thought with despair. "Or leave him alone, let him do what he wants?" Suddenly she heard a monstrous crash, and turned about. At the street corner Zawadzki had run into a man pushing his cart out of the market. The whole street was littered with apples. Zawadzki and the vendors were abusing each other so loudly that the whole street seemed to quake.

"That's a fine thing, too," she thought.

She entered the restaurant. At one time it had been owned by a gigantic sailor who weighed more than 400 pounds; now he was gone, and only caricatures that had been drawn of him remained—pictures on the wall of a colossus holding a cruiser in his hand.

Agnieszka walked up to Grzegorz. "Grzegorz," she said, "this time I haven't been looking for you. You can believe me, it's an accident."

"I believe you," he said. "Sit down."

"Grzegorz," she said. "For the first time in my life I beg you to have pity on me: go back home. I've been without sleep for so many nights that I can scarcely stand on my legs. Mother won't fall asleep, she'll have hysterics again, and I'll have to look for you again."

"She didn't come," he said.

"No," said Agnieszka. She was silent a while, then she said: "Grzegorz, you have a gun. Kill me, kill Mother, kill anyone you want, but come back home."

"One more day," he said. "If she doesn't come tomorrow, it will mean that there's no sense waiting for her any longer."

They fell silent. Then she noticed that he was saying something to her. She looked at his moving lips, but no longer understood anything. Her head was drooping, all her thoughts were confusedly woven into one—she thought of sleep. She pulled herself up suddenly. "Grzegorz," she said, "drink to my health. To my love. To Sunday."

She filled his glass. When he raised it to his mouth, she grabbed his hand in her two hands and pressed it with all her strength. The glass cracked; Agnieszka squeezed her fingers ever more tightly and felt the fragments of glass sinking into his flesh. He did not cry out; he only turned pale, and thick drops of sweat appeared on his forehead. Both watched his blood dripping on the dirty tablecloth. She squeezed her hands together so violently that her collarbone made a cracking sound.

"Come," she said.

He rose; still holding his hand and without relaxing her grip, she led him through the room out into the street. Only there did she let go of his hand. She staggered heavily and leaned against a wall. "Hit me," she whispered.

He smiled. "That was very nicely done," he said. "I thought people had been entirely sterilized, incapable of such imagination. Man's strength always flows from cruelty. That is the basis. It's a pity you've revealed yourself so late; I might have got suitable work for you before." He walked up to her, and raised her face. "Come, little one," he said. "Yes, let's go home. I'm beginning to like you for the first time."

9

When she woke, her father was already shuffling about the room in his slippers. She was still full of sleep, she was coming from very far away, when she heard a noise, and that noise—monotonous, steady—chased the remnants of sleep from her eyelids. She lay motionless, as though self-enclosed, not having the courage to open her eyes and make sure. She opened them only when she heard her father walk over to the window.

He drew the curtain and stood there, stooped over, helpless. His hand resting on the sill, he looked out into the street.

"It's raining," he said after a while. He drummed

with his fingers on the glass. "Low-lying clouds," he said. "It will rain all day."

Agnieszka threw on her robe and walked to the window. She stood beside her father. The roof glistened, water gurgled in the gutters; pedestrians were walking fast, hitching their clothes up above the wet street.

"Snow," said Agnieszka. She touched the pane. "Rain with snow. Such things can happen even in May. It was sultry all week."

"But why Sunday of all days?" her father asked despairingly. "Why must it rain on Sunday?"

"A Communist trick. To discourage people from going to church."

She dressed hurriedly and went to the kitchen. Zawadzki was shaving, whistling off key.

"Good morning," she said. "Where's Grzegorz?"

"He's gone out some place."

"Are you going?"

"Where?"

"To Julia."

"Her name isn't Julia, it's Maria," he said angrily. "Where did you hear that?"

"No matter. Are you going?"

"In this weather? Are you out of your mind?"

"What of it? You cleaned your carburetor . . ."

"I'll go next Sunday," he said. "Don't worry, I'll

fix her. There hasn't been a woman yet who could make a fool of me." He suddenly turned to her. "Why the devil are you so interested in all that?"

"You've cut yourself," said Agnieszka. "You should be careful when you shave. And I'm not a bit interested. I'm just being sociable."

Grzegorz entered the kitchen. He threw off his wet coat, sat on his bed and began to pull off his shoes.

"Are you sick?" asked Agnieszka.

"Why?"

"You're going to bed."

He raised his bloodshot eyes to her. Then he pointed to the window. "Find me something better to do."

"You might go and have a drink now," she said. "You'd be drunk by evening and go to sleep without complications."

Zawadzki walked out saying, "Have your fun without me."

Agnieszka sat on the bed next to Grzegorz. "Why don't you go now," she said. "It's all the same to you, isn't it? If you get drunk now, there's a chance you'll be run over by a streetcar or a truck. Then we'll have some peace. At night the city is empty."

"I never begin to drink before six in the afternoon," he said. "The world is going bankrupt. A man must keep his morale."

"Grzegorz," Agnieszka said, "I want to take advantage of this exceptional moment of sobriety. If you don't stop guzzling as of today, I'll go to the secretary of your party cell and tell him what you do. You shouldn't be in the party. They certainly don't need people like you."

He looked at her attentively. "You're late, little sister," he said. He patted her on the cheek. "Yesterday they took away my card." He smiled. "A wretched nation. Wretched people. They want to accomplish something at any cost, but unfortunately everything has been done before. The most you can do with my secretary is go to bed with him. Between two meetings. Is there anything else you want to tell me?"

Agnieszka was silent. She stared at the windowpane washed by the rain. The other side of the street could not be seen at all.

"Grzegorz," she said after a while, "how much of a swine can one be?"

"I'm interested in that question, too," he replied. "I have devoted myself to it entirely. When I reach my final conclusions, I'll let you know."

"Does she know about it?"

"What she?"

"That woman of yours."

"As far as I know I have no woman."

"You're waiting for her."

"I waited for other things, too. Nothing came of them." He rose suddenly. "What do you want of me? If you're looking for answers to current problems, read the *Banner of Youth*. They once conducted a discussion as to what a Young Communist's love should be like. Very instructive. The little stinkers had more to say on the subject of women than Balzac. And now let me sleep."

Their father came in. "Mother feels terrible," he said. "She has pains around her heart, she says. I've no idea what to do."

"It's best to do nothing at all," said Grzegorz. "Then at least your conscience doesn't trouble you for taking part in anything. Couldn't you discuss these world-shaking affairs out in the hall?"

Agnieszka drank her tea and went downstairs. Piotr was waiting for her in the doorway.

"Let's have a cup of coffee some place," she said. She raised the hood of her coat. "Let's not discuss that subject today. That will be best."

He nodded.

The café was crowded: they could not get a table. They took a streetcar that was headed downtown. On the front platform some drunks were fooling around;

they must have had their liquor that morning, for all of them were wearing their Sunday best.

"Do you know what?" said Piotr. "Have you ever thought about what Poland looks like?"

"What do you mean?"

"The image of France is Marianne," said Piotr. "The Americans would like the Statue of Liberty to be the symbol of their democracy. Russia was at one time represented as a bear. And what is the symbol of Poland?"

"I don't know."

"I've often thought about it," he said. "Do you know what?" He pointed to the drunks. "A fellow like that one over there, in a cheap tennis outfit. Slightly drunk. In some enormous waiting room. Without a timetable. To make the picture complete, he might be holding a copy of *King Spirit* in his left hand. A bottle in his right, for balance. Is my idea very stupid?"

"I don't know. Maybe it's stupid, maybe it's intelligent. It's raining, that's the important thing."

The downtown cafés were crowded, too. They walked from one to the other, drenched and chilled. They tried to go to a movie, but despite the rain there were long lines of people in front of them all, standing with newspapers and briefcases over their heads. At the legitimate theater, a placard announced that the performance was sold out.

"We can go somewhere to get dinner," said Agnieszka.

"I'm sorry, but I have no money. And you?"

"I haven't either. I spent all my allowance looking for Grzegorz."

"We can always go to church," said Piotr. "It's free, and there's room enough. People still love to pray. I think those various details are related. More seriously than the Lord God Himself might wish."

"Where shall we go, Pietrek?" she asked dully.

"I don't know. There's no place on earth for lovers."

They stood facing each other at some point in the wet city. They were both dripping wet. Wind-driven waves of rain kept coming down. They were spattered by passing cars, pushed by pedestrians. A woman's voice was blaring from large loudspeakers.

"Don't talk like that," she said with despair.

"I read somewhere that man's greatest unconscious wish is to become a slave," Piotr said. "I am beginning to believe it. I catch myself wanting to return to prison. Not to think, not to worry about anything. Life isn't worth living, if there is a sign 'Keep out' before every place on earth. The only thing I want is to be sentenced. The article of the code and the term don't matter to me."

He grabbed at her hands. "I'll go back there, do you hear? I'll do something that will make them put me in prison for years. I'll go back there and be done with it. We won't have to wander about any more, no one will chase us away . . ."

"Come," she said.

She took him by the hand, and almost by force dragged him after her. They walked into some ruins. She began to run without letting go of his hand; they stumbled over bricks and holes in the ground, got up again and ran on. In the end she dropped onto the ground littered with tin cans, shards of broken bottles, and sodden clay. She pulled him after her; he fell on top of her. With all her strength she grabbed his head by the hair, and pressed it to her breast. With her right hand she began to pull down his trousers. "Let's be done with it, do you hear?" she cried into his ear. "Please, don't change your mind. It doesn't matter, I tell you. People aren't any better than animals. We mustn't think we can be different. We can't do a thing about it. All we can do is put an end to this torment. Don't think about what'll happen next. Come, now, please! Come, don't run away!"

"Get away," he cried, "get away, or I'll kill you!"

"Kill me," she said. "Kill me, but afterward. Afterward, we won't be able to look at each other. And there will be peace. Peace at last. Without longing. Without love. Without Sunday. Without talk about your prison. Of course, we'll be disgusted. So what? All that isn't important. Don't run, I won't let you go. Come. Later we'll forget about each other. And there will be nothing. Now, come."

He wrenched himself free, and jumped back. Some bricks slipped, and cascaded down with a roar. For a moment he stood over her, his face dark, his hand raised to strike her. "Agnieszka," he stammered hoarsely, "Agnieszka." Then he ran down the little slope, bricks and rubble tumbling after him. She lay motionless and the water poured over her hair, her face, and her bare hips. A little while later, when she was in the street again, Piotr was gone. A small group of people had taken shelter from the rain in a doorway, and every now and then they stuck their heads out, staring up at the leaden sky. A boy kept repeating, "Damn it, damn it!" "It's all because of those bombs," someone was saying. "All because of those bombs. If they didn't explode them, the weather would be different." The whole world was full of water; one had the impression that everything was dissolving.

At home, her father stood by the window, just as he had that morning. Grzegorz was asleep in the kitchen. Agnieszka took her coat off, and sat on the couch. Her mother lay with her eyes closed.

"No fishing," said the father. "How could I go out in this rain? My God! I borrowed fifty zlotys from Lipinski for tackle, and all for nothing."

Suddenly she saw his face close to her own distorted with fury. She drew back violently, for it looked as though he were going to grab her by the throat.

"Without you," he said in a breaking voice, "without that drunk in the kitchen, I could have lived like a human being. Today, Sunday, I could have gone to see a whore, or got drunk. One day of rain, and a man's life is ruined. I must stay home and nurse your mother. I didn't go fishing, and tomorrow I'll have to shove my way into a streetcar."

Suddenly he jumped to the couch on which her mother was lying.

"Get out of that bed, you bitch," he shrieked. "Get up, die, do anything, but let it be different, let something change at last, let something change . . ."

Agnieszka was once again in the street. A boy in his teens asked her, "May I offer you my umbrella?" The dark clouds lay low, right over the roofs.

110

10

"Where did you meet Elzbieta?" the man asked.

"We studied together," said Agnieszka. "We even graduated together. Then after two years she stopped studying. I hadn't seen her since."

"And you met again only today?" he asked. He offered Agnieszka his cigaret case; she was already somewhat high, and couldn't manage to take out a cigaret. The man smiled. He extracted one and stuck it into her mouth. His hands were strong, tanned, his wrists covered with thick hair.

"Today," said Agnieszka. "I was in a doorway waiting for the rain to stop. She happened there, too, somehow. Touching, isn't it? There was once a song hit called 'Stormy Weather,' do you remember?"

He shook his head. His hair was dark, short-clipped, without sheen. A lock fell over his forehead.

"No," he said after a moment. "Please sing it. Perhaps I'll recall."

"Here? In this dive?"

He moved closer to her. She felt his breath on her neck—hot, saturated with tobacco and alcohol.

"We can go some other place," he said.

"What you mean is—to another dive."

"I didn't say that."

"Too bad. Besides, it's raining."

"I'll try to cast a spell on the sky."

"It's a pity I didn't meet you before."

"Why?"

"I'd have asked you to do it this morning."

"And now?"

"Now, it's all the same."

"To you, maybe."

"Don't you think our conversation is pretty damn stupid?"

He smiled broadly, but his eyes did not change their expression. He looked at her calmly and coldly; Agnieszka could barely endure his stare.

"Don't be too hard on us," he said. "Most people talk the way we're talking."

"And the rest?"

"I don't know. Perhaps even more stupidly."

"Yes," said Agnieszka. "Too bad I didn't know that sooner. Who is Elzbieta dancing with?"

"Some punk."

"I think it's a friend of yours."

"Rather a close one—my own brother."

He beckoned to the barman, who came up to them like one in a trance.

Agnieszka stared as the glasses filled up with a dark liquid. She bent forward a little and saw the distorted reflection of her own face in them. She drew her head back sharply.

"Let's drink," said the man.

She picked up her glass; it was very cold, covered with moisture.

"To whose health?"

"To the rain," said the man. "If it hadn't been for the rain you wouldn't have met Elzbieta. If it hadn't been for the rain Elzbieta wouldn't have brought you here. If it hadn't been for the rain I wouldn't have met you. Why don't you want to drink?"

"I'm drinking," she said. She raised her glass higher. "To the rain."

They drank. Once again the barman flashed by with the bottle. More and more people thronged around them.

"Where do you go in the summer?"

"I don't know whether I'll be able to go anywhere at all. I have to write a master's thesis. I get my degree this year."

"Master?"

"Philosophy. A profession that consists in infallibly explaining the phenomena of life. Comical, isn't it? And what are you?"

"A newspaperman. A profession that consists in writing the whole truth, the honest truth. Comical, isn't it? Of the three of us, if I'm not mistaken, Elzbieta is the best off. Just a whore. A profession without miracles or illusions."

"That's not a profession," Agnieszka said. She smiled. "That's a morality. An obvious whore— that's the highest moral status a woman can attain today."

He looked at her sideways.

"What you say has a certain freshness about it," he said. "Usually the story is different: 'When I was a young girl I met a man and I fell in love with him and he . . . and so on."

"Bah," said Agnieszka, "that's just talk. The ideal is life without illusions, without myths."

"You don't want illusions?"

"No."

114

"What *do* you want?"

"To forget," she said. "My God, if it were possible to forget. Forget father, these joints, the part of town I live in . . ."

He put his hand on her arm and drew her to him. She closed her eyes and submitted passively.

"Forget," he said softly. "Forget . . . for one day."

11

"Idiot," said the man; he was purple with rage. He pulled her head up by the hair and slapped her face twice; for a moment she felt the taste of salt. "Couldn't you find someone else for your first time? The amount of money I spent on our drinks would have got me a decent whore. Dumb cows. Even in something like this you can't be trusted."

He got into his pajamas and jumped out of bed. He pulled the blanket off her.

"This looks fine," he said. "Exactly as if I'd murdered somebody. I'll look fine, too. My wife will be back from Stalinogrod in three hours. Damn it, we've no spare sheets. What will I tell her?" He took a deep breath. "What on earth got into you? You're so good-looking, you should be an experienced whore. What have you been waiting for?"

"For the rain and for you."

"I'm sorry I flew off the handle," he said. "Excuse me, I apologize. You must help me somehow. There's hot water in the bathroom . . . Do you think these can be laundered?"

"Easily," she said. "Worse things than that can be laundered. Turn off the light, I'll get dressed."

"I don't want to see," he said furiously. He lighted a cigaret and turned away. "If only they dry in time. That cow will come in and make scenes all night long. I'd like to get some sleep, I have so much to do tomorrow . . ." He turned to her violently. "And what the devil have you been waiting for? Didn't you have some boy friend? I simply can't get it through my head!"

"I told you: I've been waiting for you."

"Now you're going to make a scene, because I seduced you, I suppose. Dammit, what's your name, anyhow?"

She burst out laughing. "No scenes," she said. She walked up to him and kissed him. "I'm very grateful to you."

"What's your name? What should I call you?"

"Anything you want. 'Darling' would be best. The

word means nothing and can be made to fit anyone. Perhaps you say it to your cat. Treasure. Sweetheart. Whore. Whorelet. Little Sun. That's good, too, isn't it? Little Sun will be best. We met during the rain, so it's because we've longed for sunshine. Everything man does, he does out of longing for a better life. Or out of a sense of moral protest. Yes. That's best— Little Sun. Help me take off that pillowcase, it'll go faster."

"Listen," he said. "Now I'm really sorry. I'm obtuse, forgive me. We must see each other, somehow. I simply can't get it through my head."

"It's nothing. Don't be upset."

"How shall we meet?"

"We won't meet at all. We'll think of each other. That'll be enough."

She washed the bed linen for him, and then she held out her hand. "Good-by," she said. "My name's Agnieszka. Agnieszka Walicka. Tell your friends about me, if you want to. And now give me twenty zlotys."

"What!"

"Twenty zlotys. For a taxi. Yes, yes. Everything must be done properly."

He drew out his wallet. "Perhaps you need more."

She shook her head. "That'll do, to begin with. Good night. My regards to your wife."

It was still raining. She could not find a taxicab anywhere; she walked through empty streets. Only an occasional window was lighted. "What time can it be?" she wondered. "Twelve? One? Two?" She had a headache. She walked with her hands in the pockets of her raincoat and her wet hair fell over her forehead. She knelt beside a puddle, and washed her hands in it. Then she rose; it took a moment before hundreds of lamps stopped whirling and settled back in their proper places. She smiled. "It's over," she thought, "now it's all over. It didn't even hurt as much as they say. The only thing I can't understand is why my nose bled. Welcome, life. Tomorrow it will surely be raining, but in a few days the weather will clear. Men will go around without coats. I'll wear a light dress, go to an ice cream parlor or to the banks of the Vistula, or leave town. Now it's filthy. Even the shadows are sticky."

She walked a long time before she reached home. A man came out of the doorway and stood before her. It was Piotr. He held out his hand. A metal object gleamed in the dim light of the street lamp.

"A key," he said in a low voice. "We've still four hours till daybreak."

She leaned against the wall. "Have you been waiting long?" she asked.

"All night," he said. "But I knew you'd come."

"What time is it now?"

He looked at his watch. "Three."

"What key is that?"

"I found an apartment," he said. "Don't ask how—by a miracle. The owner is going abroad, we can stay there some time."

"Why don't you sleep?"

"No," he said. "I've waited too long. I said to myself that the first night there I must spend with you. Let's go now."

"At seven it will be day," she said. "Maybe earlier. Maybe at six." She gripped his arm. "Listen, I want to tell you something. It may be unpleasant, but it's better than a lie. There's someone else. I've been with him a long time. I love him. Once we quarreled —it was then that I met you . . . You must forgive me. If it relieves you, you can slap me in the face. I want to go back to the other man." She suddenly pushed back his hand. "Take the key and go away."

She followed him with her eyes as he walked away. The mist and the rain muffled his steps; it seemed to her that she longed to hear them with her heart, but she heard nothing. He walked alone down the empty street—tall and slender, his head down. The street lamps drew out his shadow, and it seemed to her that he himself was a shadow gliding along the damp wilderness. He continued to hold out his hand, like a blind man; when he passed a street lamp, the key flashed. She stuck her fingers deep into her throat and bit them to keep herself from crying; her mouth was full of blood. She leaned against the wall, for the world had begun to swing dizzily. He vanished around a corner, but a moment later he re-emerged and walked toward her. She stared at him wide-eyed, but when he came close she saw that it was Grzegorz.

"What are you doing here?" he stammered. His knees were bending under him, he had to hold on to the entrance door.

"She came?" said Agnieszka.

"And went."

"Why?"

"People told her that I'd been drinking, that I drank. I said that I would keep on drinking. She returned to her husband, to bestow her pure caresses on him. With her slightly worn virtue. Now I have nothing to wait for. I can drink without illusions."

He paused.

"Nevertheless you're crying."

"But I love her," he said. "I'll always love her."

Once again he fell silent.

"Grzegorz," Agnieszka said suddenly. "Do you have your gun?"

"Why?"

"Do you have it?"

"I have."

"Come with me," she said.

"Where?"

"Close by, Grzegorz. This time, really close by. Come, but first give me that gun."

He handed it to her. She slipped the heavy metal piece into her pocket. "Let's go," she said.

He followed her. They walked a few dozen yards, turned left, and found themselves in the empty market. They walked around boxes and piles of rotting vegetables. Somewhere a dog was barking.

"Sit down," said Agnieszka. She pushed a box under him, sat next to him, and put her arm around him. "Grzegorz," she said softly, as one speaks to a little child, "you have talked to me for so many nights, now listen to me. Things in this country won't improve very soon. All of us have waited for a day that hasn't come yet. And won't come soon. It won't come in a week, in a month, or in a year. We have to wait. We must have strength. And most of all, we must live intelligently, far more intelligently than before. We must not let ourselves be deceived, we must struggle, defend ourselves against swinishness. Perhaps things will be all right later. Do you have the strength to wait, Grzegorz?"

He was silent. "Perhaps she'll come back," he said finally.

She smiled. "So what?" she said. "The novel you told me about once is a stupid fairy tale for school-children. And that woman? She'll come back or she won't come back. And suppose she does? People will throw mud at you and pull you apart again. You'll never get a chance to tell each other what binds you together and what stands between you. You'll think continually about her, about her husband, about what is going on between them at that moment . . ."

"That's enough," he said.

For a while they said nothing.

"You see," Agnieszka said after a while. She drew out the gun. For a moment she struggled with the lock, then a cartridge snapped into the chamber. "But you won't live to see all that," she said. "And when all of us are living better lives, you will be nothing. A drunken rag, a beggar who believes in nothing and in whom no one believes. Your time is up. You will be like a dead man among us . . ."

"Finish your speech," he said. "Poland was killed by speeches."

"I've finished," she said. "And beginning tomorrow I want to sleep. I want Mother to die in peace. Take this gun, the safety catch is off. Now I'll leave, and you'll do it. You won't wait for her any longer and be tormented by defeat. You won't enroll anywhere, you won't have to believe in anyone. No one will deceive you. Neither the government, nor a woman. Everything will be snuffed out. Take it."

She handed him the gun. He took it listlessly.

"One more thing," she said. "You know that I love you. Kiss me."

He bent toward her and kissed her on the cheek; his mouth was cold and hard. She shook her head.

"Not that way," she said gently. "Kiss me as if I'd never been your sister . . . Wait, I'll kiss you."

She kissed him. "Grzesio," she said, "don't think that everything is ending. Think that everything is only beginning. Everything that life should be— peace, freedom, and silence."

She walked a few steps and then ran across the market. Later, in the street, she stopped. He joined her after a few minutes.

"You knew that I wouldn't do it," he said.

She shrugged her shoulders. "Of course," she said.

"I only wanted to show you that all of us are comical with our little stories. Just comical . . ." She began to laugh. "Now you don't exist any more," she said, "nor does Pietrek. There is only the other one, with his wife from Stalinogrod. What does she look like? What does someone deceived look like? What do we all look like? There was nothing. Neither you, nor Sunday, nor anyone. There was nothing at all. To think that way is best. And now there is only freedom. That damn, crappy freedom."

She began to laugh, and kept on laughing. Later, in bed, as she listened to the breathing of her father and mother, she was still laughing. And it seemed to her that this room, this city, this world, everything was filled with laughter, which no one could hear except herself. Then it was dawn.

12

She was dressing; classes began at eight. She was about to enter the kitchen when Zawadzki came out of it. His face was solemn; he put a finger to his lips.

"Quiet," he said. "She's still asleep."

"Who's she?"

"Maria, my fiancée, well . . ."

"She arrived?"

"Didn't your parents tell you?"

"No," she said. "I came home very late last night."

He looked into her tired eyes and smiled jeeringly. "Yesterday," he said. "Last night." He smiled happily. "Those things people were saying were all lies. Life would be easier if there weren't so many kind souls around. Quiet, I think she's just got up. Grzegorz and I slept here in the hall."

They went into the kitchen. A girl sat with her back to them, combing her hair.

"Marysia," said Zawadzki, "here is Agnieszka, whom I told you about."

The girl turned around, and Agnieszka started. She was the same girl she had found with Pietrek in the flat of the young man in pajamas. "Then you looked even more innocent," Agnieszka thought. "And your eyes are of a bronze color, just as I thought."

"Good morning," Agnieszka said. "I see we're in the same boat."

Maria raised her eyebrows in surprise. "But we don't even know each other," she said.

"Never mind," said Agnieszka. "We will, and we'll help each other somehow."

"We're getting married this week," said Zawadzki. His face was radiant. "I'm going to attend to the formalities. I've had enough of separation. Congratulate us."

"I congratulate both of you," she said. "And you particularly. You've been so worried. Now, you see! Virtue is always rewarded. After all, that's what keeps the world going. Good-by. I must go to my classes."

127

Zawadzki and Maria smiled at her. She nodded. She went back to her room to get her bag. Her father stood by the window, looking out into the street.

"Low clouds," he said. "Now it will pour all week." He turned to her. "My God," he said, "my God, I wish it were Sunday."